From Russia to Rwanda with Love

From Russia
to Rwanda with Love
via other exotic places

An ordinary man's adventures with God

Written and compiled by

Richard Wallis

Published in Great Britain by

Mission Possible UK, PO Box 597, Huntingdon, Cambridgeshire
PE29 9ET

First printed December 2015

Second impression March 2016

ISBN 978-0-9935351-0-9

Cover design by Tony Fisher and text design by Roger Chouler

Printed in Great Britain by Clays Ltd., St Ives plc

About the author

After graduating with a degree in history and politics at Liverpool University in 1970, Richard lived in Zambia working with a parastatal organisation developing Zambia's rural retail infrastructure. Since returning to the UK in 1978, he has worked in the Christian charity sector holding senior positions in Scripture Union, Wesley Owen Books & Music, Signpost International and The Churches Alert against Sex Trafficking across Europe (CHASTE). In 2007 he founded Mission Possible UK.

Proceeds

Proceeds of this book will be used for the work of Mission Possible UK
www.mpuk.org

Contents

Dedication

To Him
who is able to do immeasurably more
than all we ask or imagine
according to His power that is at work within us
to Him be glory.

Ephesians 3:20

Gratitude

Getting a man to the moon was one of the great adventures of the 20th century. Neil Armstrong took that "one small step" on 21 July 1969 – but about 35000 people at NASA worked to get him there. It's true, no man is an island. We all have people to thank in our lives.

People say I am impossible to live with. Thankfully for me, Susan and Ruth proved them wrong (Proverbs 31:10). Next there are Kerry and Keith – one gave me the opportunity to have my first adventures with God, the other facilitated them. After twenty years as a Christian, they assisted me in finding my place in the Body of Christ. Since then I have been blessed by both the wisdom of the Mission Possible UK Board and the wholehearted support of my local church in Hemingford Grey. I am also very grateful for all those from around the United Kingdom who have prayed for me and have trusted Mission Possible UK with their regular and one-off giving. That is awesome. We may not have taken "one giant leap for mankind" but I believe that together we have done something beautiful for God. To Him be the glory.

And there is my thankfulness for those I have worked with overseas since 1993 – Ivo, Mirjami, Roumen and Besa in Eastern Europe, Bishop Nathan and Bishop

John in Rwanda, Pastors Peter and John Paul in Uganda, Felibien and Francois in Burundi, Matt in Brazil, Pastor Elvie Go and Bishop Ed in the Philippines and Apostle Muzamai in Zambia.

There are many others who must be included on this list – my family, those who shared the Good News of Jesus with me in a way that I could digest (not only in words), those who cared for Susan so lovingly when she was seriously ill over several years and so many more. You know who you are. I thank God for each one of you.

Richard

Introduction

This book is a hybrid. It is not an autobiography and it is not an anthology. It is a mix of both. A marketing person might call it an 'Autobiology'. It is compiled in chronological order —and yet not fully so as Chapter 3 could have sat anywhere in the first half of the book. It is a book about an ordinary man's adventures with God.

I hope this book will contribute to shattering the myth that Christianity is dull. Jesus said *'I have come that they may have life, and have it to the full'* John 10:10. Sometimes it has seemed almost too full, and I have many times experienced that strange mix of wishing I was safely back in my home whilst knowing that I am experiencing something exceedingly special. I have experienced God's provision and protection during those times.

I also hope that God will use this book to encourage people who are disheartened to ask God to instil a new passion in their hearts. You will read how God did this for me after a long period of being a 'tombstone in the pews'. He is able and to Him be the glory (Ephesians 3:20).

There are no pictures in this book. So we have set up a special page on our website and you can access pictures of stories told in this book, chapter by chapter. Simply visit **www.mpuk.org** and hit the gallery tab followed by the PowerPoint titled *'From Russia to Rwanda with Love'*.

Richard Wallis
St. Ives, Cambridgeshire
richard.wallis@mpuk.org
November 2015

Venture into the Unknown – Islands of Paradise and Poverty

'Go and make disciples of all nations'
Matthew 28:19

I had been a Christian for twenty years before I first went on mission. Of course I had done other things. I had trained as a counsellor for the 1984 Billy Graham crusades and I had completed a prayer walk from Lindisfarne to Land's End in 1986. But mission was off my radar screen.

In 1992 a group from our church had been on the first 'Walk of 1000 Men' mission walking along the Pennine Way. They came back with irresistible stories. I allowed myself to be 'volunteered' to do the second walk in Cornwall in 1993. This involved a training weekend at a church in Oxford. It was here that I had to make my first decision as a 'trainee missionary'. The arrangements were that we slept that Saturday night on the church floor. As floortime approached the instruction was given – 'snorers to the left, non-snorers to the right'. Some decisions are hard to make!

In October, we gathered in Cambridge to catch a bus to Cornwall. I was petrified. I had equipped myself with copies of 'Journey into Life', 'Four Spiritual Laws' and other booklets and poured over them as we headed towards Southampton to pick up more walkers. To my great relief the bus broke down for two hours near Heathrow Airport and momentarily I thought I would be spared the whole awful experience. A week later I returned home enthused with my own stories.

One other volunteer act defined 1993 as a watershed year in my life. Our assistant minister Kerry had been to the Philippines and returned with his own stories of God at work in shanty towns and villages in remote mountain regions. I volunteered to a run child sponsorship programme for the mission society that he founded as a result of his trip – Signpost International. He handed over a file with 900 photographs of Filipino children looking for sponsors. We never found sponsors for all 900 but we were soon supporting several hundred children. Gradually it dawned on me that I would need to visit the Philippines. We departed Stansted on a cold morning early in December 1994. This was to be my first adventure with God – and an extreme one it was too.

'You can feel a gentle sea breeze on your face and warm sand between your toes as you listen to the gentle lapping of waves' exuded the travel brochures on the Philippines comprising more than seven thousand islands in the Western Pacific. The beauty of these islands is spectacular. But staying in an urban slum, amongst poverty, malnutrition, disease and death, shocked me. On the first morning, I visited some of the sponsored children. Stilt houses ran all along the bay linked together by rickety bridges stretching out well into the sea. They live here because a large city is good for casual work but they cannot afford to rent houses on land. The smell is unforgettable as you navigate the 'bridges' – to me more like rope bridges – moving from house to house further out to sea. Each home has a direct toilet to the shore below. The flush happens only when the tide comes in. Further hazards are huge fires that often destroy many of these homes clustered so close together; homes which also take the brunt of the many typhoons that approach from across the sea. We call them slums and shanties, they call them home.

I had not had time to take stock of my feelings – largely ones of outrage – when we were off to the city prison. Soon I was facing four cages similar to those you see at zoos – except in this case there were about twenty prisoners in each cage. I asked what we were doing there. I was told that we would sing a few songs and then I would preach. I had never preached before and had not prepared anything. I was about to try my 'wriggling out of a tight spot' technique when a sentence came to mind: 'I was once condemned to death'. Maybe that would give me some 'street cred' with the prisoners. I preached. And I discovered one thing on that first day about mission. Be prepared. Living on mission can be a bit like being a spitfire pilot. There are long periods when nothing happens but you never know when the call to scramble will come. And on this trip, the call to scramble came in many ways including leading a Bible study in the dingy central market; pre-dawn evangelism in the slum areas which started by singing outside people's houses to wake them and being guest of honour at a birthday party.

After a few days we moved onto another island and from urban poverty to rural poverty. Our ship docked in General Santos City on Mindanao Island in the Southern Philippines at dawn after our twenty hour voyage. I had slept little. Economy class featured wobbly iron bunk beds nailed to the deck! Roosters in cardboard boxes crowed all night. Then towards dawn armed guards took up their stations around the boat. We were passing by the Zamboanga Peninsula where an insurgency was underway. But dawn brought a stunning sight – clear blue water with flying fish, palm tree rimmed golden beaches and a magnificent volcano on the horizon. But this was not to be a day for lazing on a beach. I was on my first mission trip to a remote mountain region eighty miles northwest of the city.

One joy of mission is that you travel with locals rather than with tourists. We took a rickety bus full of chattering Filipinos to the foot of the mountain range and then a jeepney into the mountains. Jeepneys are unique to the Philippines – a sort of exceedingly colourful and ornate jeep with a roof. People piled into the jeepney while I joined others sitting on the roof rack and enjoyed being bounced around on the potholed dirt road. This was in the days before risk assessments! Up and up we climbed into the mountains until we reached a narrow track on our right. We followed this on foot to reach the village we were visiting. Our luggage was placed on a wooden sledge which was dragged along by a cow – wheels were useless on these rutted paths. After walking for almost an hour in light mountain drizzle – I discovered that banana leaves make great umbrellas – we reached a bamboo house on stilts in an isolated valley. This was to be our home for the next few days.

It was back to basics. No electricity, so nothing to do after dusk except sit around a single candle and talk. A pit latrine with walls made of sack was located behind the bamboo house – at night one had to negotiate numerous large bull frogs to reach it. Bed was a mat on the bamboo floor. The bathroom was the nearby stream. We ate off the land. One afternoon as I was relaxing, I heard a piercing squeal. I will never forget the sound. They were slaughtering a pig for the meal that evening. As we sat down to eat our pork chops three hours later, the head of the pig was hanging from a beam looking at us.

We visited the homes of subsistence farmers. Without exception, we were warmly welcomed and had many opportunities to share the good news of Jesus. I remember praying one morning for Ninfa – a young woman seriously ill and expected to die. Some months later, I was told that God had completely healed her. I preached again at a special celebration meeting in the packed bamboo built church – so packed that one wall collapsed as I was speaking! And I discovered the ministry of 'simply being there'. People living in remote places can feel forgotten. Having visitors who care enough to travel thousands of miles to visit them can be a massive encouragement. As one whispered to me as I was preparing to leave – 'You bothered to come. That is important to us. Thank you brother.' I thought for a second and then whispered back 'Thank you brother for welcoming me. Living in your community has been a life changing experience for me'.

At the end of the visit, our trip back to the base of the mountains included bareback riding on the local ponies and a crazy dirt road motorbike ride with four passengers. Motorbike taxis on Mindanao are called 'Skylabs' and their drivers are true masters. It is humbling to observe the balance, technique and skill of these riders.

This should have been the end of our adventure on Mindanao. The film *Romancing the Stone* came to mind when I thought of our travel over the past few days. But more was to follow. The ferry we had booked to catch out of General Santos City had been cancelled and the next one was not due for seven days. That would not get us home in time for Christmas. As a result of the cancellation, all the seats on Philippines Airlines had been taken while we were in the mountains. So we checked into some local accommodation where the rooms were small and like prison cells with no windows – just an air brick. Then I had a brilliant idea. Let's charter a flight. We walked up to the airport and saw some light aircraft there. I asked for contact details and phoned the number. A gruff voice said he would call into our lodgings to see us at 8 pm. When he had not appeared by 9.30pm, we retired to our rooms for much needed sleep. Then at 10.30 pm there was an urgent knock on the door. Some people had come to see us. It does not take long to dress in warm climates and within seconds I was downstairs where I was greeted by a huge man with four minders standing in each corner of the room. This guy was no commercial pilot. He slid a bottle of beer across the table to where I was seated. Realising that this was not the time to discuss the 4 D's of mission (no dating, no drinking, no drugs, no driving), I assessed the situation quickly. We were in hot water. We had moved from *Romancing the Stone* to a scene from *The Godfather*. Not wishing to find a horse's head in my bed, we agreed to meet again the following day to negotiate a price. But the following morning we thought better of it, checked out of the accommodation and moved elsewhere in the city. We were deluding ourselves that we could hide from this man. So it was to our massive relief that we heard from Philippines Airlines that our standby request had been converted into a confirmed booking. This adventure was coming to an end and we would be home in time for Christmas after all!

James Bond, Lamborghinis and Fur Coats

*'Whatever you did for one of the least of these brothers
and sisters of mine, you did it for me'*
Matthew 25:40

*Possibly this is the most unusual chapter heading that you have found
in a book on mission. Read on!*

*In May 1998, I was invited as a delegate to a conference
on 'Children at Risk' at Ashburnham Place in Sussex. By this
time I was not only running the child sponsorship programme and
spearheading a house building programme in the Philippines but was
also due to visit Matt Roper who had a street girl project in Brazil
(See chapter 4).*

*I was slightly fearful about the conference as by nature I am shy
and knew none of the other hundred or so delegates. I know it sounds
absurd but what do you do, for example, at mealtimes. Do you go
into the dining room first hoping that someone will sit beside you or
do you go in last and hope you can gate crash into a conversation
between people who already know each other? I am a shy extrovert.*

*My fears at this conference were justified. Not only did I not
know anyone else but everyone else had such powerful testimonies. I
was a fish out of water. And then I saw this bear! He looked like a
bear out of honey. A possible soulmate?*

*The bear was bearded Ivo Ivanov, a Bulgarian, who was raised
in the underground church in Bulgaria. He had to flee that country
as a persona non grata and eventually ended up in Finland where
initially he smuggled Bibles into Russia with his wife Mirjami.*

21

When that seemed 'too much like hard work', Ivo started stripping down printing presses and smuggling those into Russia piece by piece, so Bibles could be printed in-country! Another powerful testimony but, at the conference, someone like me on his own and looking for a friend. So it was that Ivo invited me to Russia. I accepted and in December 1998, left Stansted again, this time for Helsinki.

To the Finland Station is a book by Edmund Wilson presenting the history of revolutionary thought from the French Revolution to the arrival of Lenin at the Finlyandsky Rail Terminal in St. Petersburg in 1917. As someone who had studied politics at university, I felt 'the hand of history on my shoulder' as we pulled out of the station in Helsinki following the same route Lenin took some eighty years before. And yet, as we got to the border crossing with Russia at midnight, I was not thinking of Lenin but James Bond! For someone who had lived through the cold war, travelling by train to Russia seemed something out of fiction – not so much *From Russia with Love* as 'to Russia with Love'.

And I might as well get the 'fur coats' bit out of the way at this stage. I was wondering what my first impression would be as we arrived in Moscow on that freezing December day. It was fur coats. My eyes almost popped out. Everyone was wearing fur coats. It was as if I was on the set of my favourite film as a teenager – *Doctor Zhivago*.

The journey gave Ivo plenty of time to share with me about the work of Mission Possible. The political transition in Eastern Europe opened up an historic opportunity for this mission organisation. Odessa which had already been

Mission Possible's base from which four million Bibles were distributed into the former Soviet Union now became a strategic base for new activities. An education centre was opened to train over 1000 indigenous church planters who returned to different parts of the former Soviet Union. Alongside this, a three year Bible Study correspondence course was launched that still runs to this day. And finally there was an important Train the Trainers conference for Sunday school teachers. The delegates at this conference afterwards trained 8000 Sunday School teachers across these territories – so important, as children's ministry had hitherto been forbidden.

However, we were not on the way to any conference centre but to the streets of St. Petersburg and Moscow. As a result of the economic upheavals in the early 1990s hundreds of thousands of children and teens ended up on the streets. One day Ivo saw a boy holding a sign saying *'I am hungry, please help me'*. Ivo knew he had to respond to this plea. The first street patrol was launched in the winter of 1995 visiting Moscow railway stations where homeless children were staying despite temperatures as low as -30°C.

I met Diana on the trip. Diana earned her living at a rail station in Moscow as a street merchant because her mother was unemployed. Diana would boast of her early days on the street by bragging 'I collect more money than most boys and could handle vodka better than they could too.' Later Diana was kidnapped by a street gang to be used as their 'slave'. Eventually her brother Boris seized her back and they made their way to Mission Possible's shelter home that had recently been established. She had some serious catching up to do at school but she was a dedicated student. In 2005 she graduated from school and went on to study law. Now she is happily married with children. As Diana now says *'My life was at a dead end. But after the Christian people started to look after me, everything changed. Today I am a Christian and believe that with God, nothing is impossible'*.

Mission Possible purchased a farm near Yaroslavl about an hour's drive north east of Moscow. Ivo was keen that I saw this, so we left early, having borsch for breakfast on the way. I had never seen borsch on a Little Chef breakfast menu – no surprise perhaps as the main ingredient is beetroot. What would I have given for an all-day breakfast! The original purpose of the farm was to provide food for the growing number of shelter homes but the vision soon extended. There was little point in seeking to integrate the children found on the streets back into their families if there was violence and abuse at home. Substance abuse from vodka to glue is a massive problem in Russia. The farm was an ideal place for a rehabilitation centre and rehabilitants were given the opportunity to gain self-esteem by working on the farm. And this is where the Lamborghini comes into our story. Someone donated a Lamborghini tractor to the farm. So unless you know differently, Mission Possible is the only charity with a Lamborghini! The farm is a place of surprises and to me one of the most wonderful things is that after a long harsh winter, they cannot wait to break the ice on a local river and baptise many of the rehabilitants.

Given my experience in child sponsorship, this was one obvious response to my visit and we started a new programme. But as a Christian bookseller, I had a passion to do something else as well. So we found funding to provide libraries for hundreds of new churches that had been established as a result of the training ministry in Odessa. These were shipped from Moscow to remote parts of Russia. If only each of these books could tell their own story…

Nine years later, there was one totally unexpected outcome of this visit. Having left Signpost International, I was considering founding a new mission society to support those I had previously worked with in Africa – calling it *'Changing Lives'*. My vision was a small relational mission society adhering to the values I hold. Ivo asked if I would consider expanding the geographical areas of this new charity to include Eastern Europe. In turn, I asked him if I could use the name Mission Possible in the UK as I liked the name. And so, on this mutually agreed basis, *Mission Possible UK (MPUK)* was founded in March 2007. The mission of MPUK is to advance the Christian faith by serving the poor, forgotten and marginalised through serving children and families at risk, training Christian leaders and distributing Christian literature. Mission Possible UK (MPUK) is independent of but in fellowship with Mission Possible in Eastern Europe and unlike them we also work in Africa.

Stories from Around the World – My Chapter

'For God gave us a spirit not of fear but of power and love and self-control'

2 Timothy 1:7

It had never been my intention to write for publication. My profession was a bookseller and not an author. From 1993 to 2009 I was responsible for author tours and special event bookstalls at events such as Spring Harvest, Keswick and Greenbelt for Wesley Owen Books & Music (WO). I combined this with overseas mission. Wesley Owen's holding company Send the Light not only released me to do this but also, amazingly, funded me. In early 2002, the Group Chief Executive Keith Danby invited me to write a chapter for a book to be titled Stories from Around the World. *I declined his invitation and that book went on to sell an overwhelming 63000 copies in the 4 months after publication in September 2002 – a runaway bestseller.*

So in early 2003 it was decided to publish Stories Around the World 2 *and once again I was invited to write a chapter. I felt it would be churlish not to consider doing this in the light of the support that Send The Light were giving to support my mission activities. And two things prompted me to say 'yes' this time. First, I had just returned from a mission trip to a refugee camp in Tanzania which proved to be another adventure with God and second my sister decided to celebrate her 60th birthday taking the family for a week long holiday on a remote farm in Devon in freezing February. What else was there to do with all that down time except write a chapter!*

Stories Around the World 2 *proved to be another bestseller – though I do not take the credit as you have to get to page 200 before you discover 'my chapter'! I was not sure there was enough on my trip to Tanzania to reach my word count quota, so I prefixed this story with a bit of my personal testimony*

It was difficult to decide where to place this chapter in this book. This book seeks to progress in chronological order but this chapter starts in 1973 and ends in 2007. So there was a case to put this chapter at the start of the book or towards the end. I have compromised by putting it here!

Led to Zambia 1973

I might never have gone to Africa had I caught my usual train that summer morning in 1972. I was working as a young department manager at the huge Owen Owen store in Liverpool (I might as well admit at this point, somewhat embarrassed, that I was in charge of ladies' gloves, handbags and hosiery). I didn't know what had possessed me to catch the bus and the ferry from my bedsit in New Brighton to Liverpool Pier Head to work instead of taking my usual train to Liverpool Central. The balding executive sitting in front of me on the bus had left his copy of the Daily Telegraph. Now I could check what was on TV that evening! But as I settled on to a deck seat on the ferry, I noticed the paper was folded to the appointments page, and there it was – 'Retail Managers required in Zambia'. Though not yet a Christian, I thanked God.

I felt sure this was the opportunity I was looking for to experiment with some ideas I had developed during my time at Liverpool University studying politics, specialising in the culture of poverty. Within a month, I was attending an interview in London. I had told no one. The day after my interview God spoke to me! One of my hosiery consultants, Debbie, was ill and her mother phoned to let me know. She then added, 'The Lord has a message for you.' I was completely bemused and asked, 'Lord who?' Her mother laughed. 'God! And he told me a great opportunity will come your way later this week and he says you must take it.' I took it. A contract, a successful first driving test, a work permit, my first passport and X-ray plates (to prove I did not suffer from TB), and I was on a plane for the first time – destination Chingola, on the Copperbelt. Rarely could a person have left to spend five years in Africa so ill equipped. I had only travelled to France and Germany, and my retail experience was limited to stockings and mittens!

However, I was full of idealism and passion. Having just seen David Lean's film *Lawrence of Arabia*, I was somehow going to become 'Wallis of Africa' and change the world. Big dreams cost nothing. So began my mini social experiment in the ZCBC store in Chingola, managing a staff team of sixty Zambians. Never had they seen a 'musungu' (white man) mopping the floors after work, nor had the company van been used to run staff back to the townships in the evenings. Never had a store manager offered to conduct free evening classes or refereed inter-departmental football matches.

One evening, after I had been in Zambia for about four months, one of my staff challenged me. 'Richard, you are a good man. You want to change the world. But you will never change the world. Only changed hearts will change the world and only Jesus can change hearts.' Five days later, I turned my vehicle over several times on a dirt road and plunged into a deep culvert. Squeezing out of the smashed rear window of the crushed car, one of my shaken but unhurt passengers whispered, 'Richard, at least I knew where I would have been going if the car had gone up in flames.' Unknown to me, members of a local church had chosen that very week to meet together at six o'clock each morning to pray for me. Talk about being chased by God! Within a week, I was an 'African' Christian.

No messages received – the 1980's

Those five years as a young Christian in Zambia were a euphoric time, but sometimes God's voice isn't so loud and clear. During those years of childlike adventures abroad, I had married Susan, who I had first met on the infamous Liverpudlian handbag counter. I thought I would have to 'grow up' on returning to England in 1978 with our two children, Christopher and Anna. And coming back home was a huge culture shock. Our third child, Sarah, soon followed and I struggled as I faced the reality of both family and work responsibilities – the inevitable mortgage, the pressures of managing Scripture Union's chain of bookshops, leaving home before six a.m. to commute to London, trying to be an effective father. More and more, I felt like a tombstone when sitting on the pews of my local church. Increasingly exhausted, the passion was gradually being squeezed out of me. Both the bookshop chain and my family grew and flourished, but it somehow felt like I was marking time.

God uses ministers – 1990 and 1993

Eventually, after ten years, and by now scared that life would continue like this, the tombstone went to see his vicar. I told him that I felt that I was past my sell-by date as a retail executive and he asked what I wanted to do with the rest of my life. I had no clear idea, but what mattered most to me was not what I did, but rather having a passion for something. He shared something that proved a wise insight. We expect too much from God over a one-year period, but too little over seven years. But could God rekindle this fire? Did God still have a plan for a life that at forty-two seemed derailed? I would be forty-nine in seven years – I was convinced it was all too late.

Then a new assistant minister, Kerry Dixon, arrived at our church. He told Susan that one day I would be a Bible teacher. That sounded ludicrous to me. All he had heard was me reading the lesson! He had no idea how desperately I tried to avoid any public speaking. Six months later, Kerry led a team, which included Susan, to the shanty towns of the Philippines. While I was grappling with increasingly grim sales figures, a result of the recession of the early nineties, they were encountering Third World poverty and were seeing God at work in ways they had not experienced before.

Six months later, over a drink with Kerry on a riverbank, I found myself volunteering to assist him on a child sponsorship programme that he had initiated.

The first package I received contained photographs of 900 Filipino children. I was overwhelmed but soon over a hundred children were sponsored and I realised I needed to visit the Philippines.

God uses shanty girls

It was on that trip that I met one of our sponsored children, Cheryl Lynn de Juan. An eight-year-old girl with a father earning less than a dollar a day was about to transform the life of a forty-six-year-old man earning almost a hundred times more. She lived in squalid and crowded conditions in a tumbledown shack built on stilts above the sewage of a large Filipino coastal shanty town. I was outraged. The night before returning home, I was sharing a room with two others in Manila. By two in the morning I could contain it no longer and shouted, 'It has happened, it has happened, it has happened!' Stirring from their sleep, the other two asked, 'What has happened?' I retorted, 'I have the passion!' Now I had a purpose.

The visit to my vicar had eventually resulted in an answer: God had used that grim shanty town to burn his passion for the poor into my heart. And I knew that when I returned to the UK, I would have to spearhead a housing project to relocate some of these families. I became the first employee of a small Cambridgeshire Christian charity working with the poor. It was only later that I realised that this coincided with the seven year anniversary of that meeting with my vicar. God's hand often appears more visible with hindsight.

"This is Mission Control calling": 2000

I sat at my desk as dusk fell on 31 December 1999 and realised how much had been achieved in a short time. Projects had been initiated in Uganda and Rwanda, including a new secondary school in Kigali; and a partnership was formed with Mission Possible, which works with street children in Moscow. Christian resource centres were established in Uganda and Rwanda. In the Philippines, we started a new micro loan project, initiated more housing projects and a Bible college was established. I reflected on Ephesians 3:20.

However, I had one concern that evening. Susan's health was deteriorating. In July 1999 she had resigned as a nurse. Here was one of the most active women I have ever met, with a big heart for mission, going through what appeared to be the most traumatic menopause of all time. It was suggested that an extended period working as a nurse with a medical mission on the Amazon would re-fire her. She left for the Amazon Basin in July 2000 and I joined her in November for her final few weeks there. As I landed on an airstrip in the middle of the rainforest, I knew this would be a significant reunion, but I was not prepared for a reunion with a wife who had become like a dependent child with severe learning difficulties. Looking back, it is amazing I did not panic.

What was wrong with Susan? Why was she constantly hallucinating? Should I return home the following day with her? Why had I not been warned? Instead of panicking, this most undomesticated of men learned to cook, started to clean and even became proud of his whites! This husband who had been cared for all his married life now became the carer. In the midst of this complete role reversal in the rainforest, I encountered God. To my utter astonishment, I felt he was calling me to teach the rural poor. The thought of teaching made this activist feel vulnerable and this vulnerability only increased when I was told that Susan was suffering from the degenerative Pick's disease – a form of premature dementia, which had started five years earlier when she was just fifty.

Mission control: "All systems go!": 2002

It was in a grand library at a theological college in London on a frosty January morning in 2002 that I met François Nitunga. There are some people you feel privileged to meet and God knows when we are in need of an inspiring encounter. But this Burundian refugee did not strike me as a particularly impressive man as I struggled to understand what the delegates were talking about. However, I am glad to say my first impression was wrong. After the meeting, he invited me to lead a mission in a Burundian refugee camp in Tanzania, close to the Burundian border.

Once again, God seemed to be propelling me forward 'despite' – despite my totally disorganised prayer life, despite my inadequacies, despite Susan's illness. Maybe grace has a whole deal to do with 'despite'. Rarely could a person have left on a teaching mission in Africa with so little experience. I had never been to Bible school and had no teaching track record. I was no longer just an idealist, but an idealist without illusions. I was no longer inspired by just a film but by an encounter with God to bring a message of hope to the oppressed.

I had travelled overseas a good deal and had survived some tight spots. I had been apprehended by the police in Belo Horizonte, who had thought I was kidnapping a street child, and just twenty-four hours later almost drowned on the Copacabana. On Mindanao in the Philippines I had been flattened to the ground by a church leader in order to avoid some passing Muslim terrorists and in Rwanda had crossed a bridge charged with sticks of volatile dynamite. Once I had even stupidly been the cause of international tensions along an African border. So I was surprised to find myself so anxious before this particular trip. My mission partner, Pastor Stuart Merton, and I were to link up with François in Nairobi, the capital of Kenya. The week before I departed, there was a missile attack on an Israeli charter flight on the Kenyan coast. Two days before, the British High Commission in Nairobi closed due to a terrorist threat. Suddenly I wished I had not booked a direct flight from Heathrow to save time – a British Airways jumbo jet now looked very big and very British.

As we prepared to land on a warm and sunny African morning I wondered about the local security arrangements; in particular, would the Kenyan Army be patrolling under the flight path? But I was staggered to see that as soon as we touched down we were surrounded by heavily armed jeeps racing either side of our aircraft and that there were armed soldiers every fifty metres on each side of the runway. As we slowed to a halt, the pilot announced that we would be taken to a special secure part of the airport. Clearly we were a target. Then the pilot added, 'We have a special guest with us today, as one of our passengers is President Daniel arap Moi!' And so I was welcomed back to Africa with a red carpet, a guard of honour, a military band and dancing ladies!

Nairobi is not Africa – at least not the Africa I love. Thankfully, we were soon in a six-seater aircraft flying to Mwansa on the southern shores of Lake Victoria where we transferred to an older six-seater to take us to Ngara on the Tanzania–Burundi border. The second pilot was one of those colourful characters who add so much to an African adventure. He was appalled by the amount of luggage we were travelling with and, having carefully weighed both his customers and their luggage, prepared for take-off. He ended his take-off checklist with 'and if all else fails, bail out in Lake Victoria'. Later he made me promise that François would not return with the entire Burundian tea harvest in sacks. I got the message. Next time I will forget the toothbrush.

The scenery was stunning – it was rainy season and the lush green hills rose to almost 6000 feet, separated by deep valleys. Our base was a settlement on top of one of these hills, called Murgwanza, as visitors were not allowed to sleep at the refugee camp. The settlement was given to the Anglicans when they arrived in 1932, as this highest hill was considered 'cursed'. Cursed it might have been, but it has magnificent views across a valley to the hills of Burundi and Rwanda. Today, the hill boasts a cathedral, mission hospital and primary school. Living conditions were basic in this remote spot and lying in bed, exhausted, each night I wondered if those 1932 pioneers had carried my bed with them on their backs all the way from Dar es Salaam. Before dawn each morning I would hear the rustle of our Tanzanian hosts stoking up the fire, so that hot water was ready in a bucket for the early morning shower. It was truly loving hospitality from such an impoverished people.

The refugee camp was about twenty-five miles from Murgwanza. The Dean of the Cathedral decided to be our taxi driver. He certainly had the knowledge! He was a delightful Christian full of the joy of the Lord in spite of one big problem − his Datsun pickup was terminally sick. I know little about vehicles, but I know when one is dying. We always travelled with our personal mechanic perched in the back; he was called on to perform operations on various parts of the body every few miles. This was all very amusing until one day we were told we would need to travel in convoy with a police escort as there were bandits in the area. Within a few minutes the convoy with armed escort had disappeared over the horizon as we spluttered along trying to negotiate a small hill. Suddenly every boulder along the roadside looked like a potential bandit road-block. Adventures with God are an exhilarating mixture of fear and expectation.

I have a vivid imagination, and for weeks had been trying to visualise a camp with 200,000 refugees. I had been invited to visit two refugee camps earlier in 2002 when on a trip to Goma in the Congo, where thousands had been displaced by a lava flow swamping the city centre. Each of these was a newly established, tented camp with 3000 refugees. But 200,000 is a figure of 'biblical proportions'. I envisaged a camp with a constant swirl of humanity, like rush hour on the London Underground, all bathed in a sort of mystical dust! This excited me as I reflected on the crusades that had been planned. But my first impression of Lukole could not have been more different: mud-brick houses in neat rows, dirt roads which were wide tree-lined avenues, an air of permanence, a measured pace of life. It was a complete contrast from the congested chaos of the shanty towns I had visited in the Philippines or in the African cities of Kampala, Lusaka and Nairobi.

Extraordinarily, my first impression was that of a suburb in the middle of the African bush. And gradually it dawned on me that it had not just an air of permanence but was a place of permanence. The first Burundian refugees arrived after the 1972 genocide with further large influxes from Burundi in 1993 and from Rwanda during the 1994 genocide. Many of the young adults in the camp must have been born there. Like their parents, they largely depend on food handouts from the UNHCR. Worse, they are not permitted to travel more than four kilometres from the camp, and even this small distance was technically illegal; they are 'prisoners' in this bush suburb. Five per cent of all Burundians are 'prisoners' here. Despite fear of violence at night in the camp, each person I spoke to had a much deeper fear of returning to his or her homeland.

François Nitunga is one of the new generation of young Christian leaders who keep pressing on towards a goal despite seemingly insurmountable obstacles. I had also noted this quality in Nathan Amooti, Director of Education for the Kigali diocese, who I had met in Rwanda a few years earlier. We had sent him a few thousand pounds to start construction of the first diocesan secondary school. As soon as I landed, he proudly took me to the site near the airport. I inspected a low wall emerging from the foundations of a small classroom block. To my astonishment, Nathan announced, 'We will start recruiting staff next week and will open in September.' I was travelling with a headmaster from Cambridge and he almost choked. Funds for the building were almost exhausted and it was touch and go if this small building would have a roof by September. There were no funds for salaries, textbooks or even school desks. Despite our concerns, Nathan pressed on, and the school opened in September, educating many who would have left school after primary education. Since those early days, God has provided funds beyond my vivid imagination, and today the school is an impressive complex educating 300 Rwandans. Like Nathan, François has a dream, and continues when most of us would give up. His dream is to prepare a people in exile to return as 'society changers' to their homeland. And what are the obstacles? A people afraid of returning home, the increasing influence of Islam in the area, the potential decimation of a generation through the Aids pandemic and a critical shortage of funds. Just one of these would have grounded me. François had asked Stuart Merton and me to train leaders on subjects related to overcoming some of these obstacles – the uniqueness of Jesus, the need for forgiveness and reconciliation, hope, evangelism, discipleship and a call for excellence in Christian leadership. In the afternoons, there were open-air crusades. The stories of these refugees were painfully similar.

The story of one young man I spoke to echoed the experiences of many. 'The militia came to our school one night in 1993 and started to wreck the place and then killed many of my school friends. I managed to squeeze out of the back window of the dormitory and ran away into the bush. God protected me as I travelled to Tanzania. I heard later that my parents and younger brothers had been killed in our home a few weeks after I reached the refugee camp. The authorities may send me back to Burundi, and I am very frightened by that prospect, as I fear I will be killed by the militia if I return.'

I was asked to preach in a packed church on Sunday morning. I felt a little emotional when I first awoke to the sounds of the 'hot water makers', remembering that my daughter, Sarah, would be in a refugee camp in Thailand that same Sunday; she was working there. The pastor asked, 'If anyone is here for the first time, please stand up.' Among the few who stood up was a seventy-year-old woman. As she spoke, there was a sudden hush in the church, followed by cries of joy. She was the wife of the elderly church treasurer who had fled from Burundi in 1993. She had crossed the Tanzania–Burundi border with their niece the previous night. They had been out of touch for nine years and there had been the possibility that they would never meet again. This was a wonderful reunion. It was a poignant reminder to me before I preached of the suffering that there is in the camp. It also made me realise how important it was to say that although I may not fully understand these people's suffering, Christ (himself a child refugee as a result of genocide and later betrayed by a close friend before suffering on the cross) most certainly does. There had been no repatriation of the Burundian refugees but the repatriation of the Rwandans from the camp was almost complete.

On our final day, a convoy of about 20 lorries came to collect about 3500 refugees. As I watched the convoy depart, I noticed something on the last lorry. It looked like a skip at our local refuse collection centre – rickety chairs, soiled plastic buckets, bags stuffed with rags, old pots and so on. Then reality struck me – it represented the worldly wealth of these 3500 refugees as they returned to face an uncertain future.

God still had a few more surprises in store. Our light aircraft landed at Nairobi's domestic airport during a massive tropical thunderstorm. On the way to the international airport our taxi broke down in a flash flood in the middle of an extremely busy highway. Was I really going to die in a huge puddle on a highway in some foreign land? Suddenly a lorry trying to overtake us by going on to the central reservation jack-knifed around us. God protected us from all the speeding traffic by giving us shelter in the armpit of the lorry and trailer. And I had 'survived' my first teaching mission to Africa.

Postscript

Much has happened since I wrote the above in 2003

Susan died in June 2005. She could not speak for the last two years of her life and by 2004 was suffering from motor neurone as well as Pick's disease. Many would have called her a 'vegetable' but throughout her illness you could clearly see Jesus in her – she was an amazing witness with a team of loyal carers who ensured she remained at our home throughout her illness. The following year proved to be a tough year but 2007 was a year of new beginnings. In March 2007, we launched Mission Possible UK working in Africa and Eastern Europe with the twin objectives of serving children and families at risk and equipping Christian leaders – the two passions God has given me now in one new mission society. Then in May 2007, I married Ruth – another beautiful Christian woman. Ruth has been a wonderful co-worker as we have seen God do exceedingly more through Mission Possible UK than either of us could have dreamt or imagined.

I am challenged by the words of Theodore 'Teddy' Roosevelt, President of the United States in the early part of last century. His words remind me of the inspirational Christian leaders I have worked alongside in Africa, Eastern Europe and Asia over the past twenty years. Whereas we often baulk at taking risks fearing failure, they keep on persevering in the most difficult and challenging situations where I would have almost certainly given up.

It is not the critic who counts: not the person who points out how the man stumbled or where the doer of deeds could have done better. The credit belongs to the man who is actually in the arena: whose face is marred by dust and sweat and blood; who strives valiantly; who errs and comes short again and again, because there is no effort without error or shortcoming; who does actually try to do the deed; who knows the great enthusiasms, the great devotions and spends himself in a worthy cause; who at worst, if he fails, at least fails while daring greatly.

Far better it is to dare mighty things, to win glorious triumphs even though chequered by failure, than to rank with those poor spirits who neither enjoy nor suffer much because they live in the grey twilight that knows neither victory nor defeat. (Theodore Roosevelt)

Street Girls – Hope on the Streets of Brazil

'You turn my wailing into dancing; you remove my sackcloth and cloth me with joy'

Psalm 30:11

The months from December 1998 to August 1999 were months of extraordinary adventures with God. These months saw my first visit to four countries – Russia (December) Brazil (March) Rwanda (July) and Uganda (August).

Matt Roper is one of those outrageously gifted people who has drifted in and out my life at roughly five year intervals. In 1998, he had founded a ministry called Meninadança – established to reach out to the street girls of Belo Horizonte, to offer them a place of security and safety, rehabilitation and re-integration into society. The project was called Meninadança as in Portuguese this means 'Dance Girl' and dance is a significant way for the self-esteem of the girls to be built up.

I had been asked, at short notice, to fly out to Brazil both to encourage Matt and also to report back on how this new ministry was developing. I left Gatwick on a long daylight flight to Rio. By the time I arrived in Rio I was exceedingly tired. Matt was supposed to meet me at the airport but was nowhere to be seen. Then I did one of the big 'no nos' at any international airport. A man came up to me and asked if I was looking for a taxi. I said yes and was led to a side area. As soon as I got into the taxi, I realised I had been a fool but it was too late. You can imagine how horrified I was when after a couple of miles, the driver said he needed to get something out of the boot. My mind went into overdrive. This was Rio, not my hometown in Cambridgeshire. Then he came back into the driver's seat, turned around and offered me a cold beer!

Matt had booked me into cheap lodgings in the red light district – I guess he wanted to prove to me that he understood cost control, knowing that one of my concerns was the cost of the Meninadanca project. At the reception desk, they told me he was in a restaurant in Ipanema. I could not resist going to Ipanema (did it really exist!) despite my tiredness and the lateness of the evening. As another taxi driver drove me there, I saw for the first time the magnificence of the statue of Christ. Some tourist attractions disappoint – this one certainly did not. The following day, Matt drove me to Belo Horizonte where I was amazed by his ministry. Possibly I could not have been safer than with Matt. The street children not only knew him but respected him too. After my week there, I knew Matt had a book in him but how was I to get him to write one. So the following year when Matt returned to the UK for a break, I took him down to Minehead, 'locked' him in a hotel room and told him to write while I walked on Exmoor. The result was Street Girls *which became an instant bestseller at the number one spot in the Christian book charts for several months in 2001.*

The following is an extract from Chapter 5 of this book. As you will read, my trip ended on the same 'adventurous' note as it had started. And there is one additional thing that Matt is still unaware of: I had a few hours in Rio before the flight left for Gatwick, so I headed down to the Copacabana beach. The surf was superb and I enjoy body surfing. But I had not reckoned on the waves being so much more powerful than in Cornwall. Soon I had been turned turtle and sandpapered my forehead. Sporting a significant raw area I looked as if I had been in a brawl. And I am still staggered that the airline allowed me on their flight home a few hours later.

I pulled my sweater over my knees and hugged my legs tightly as I crouched on the cold, concrete steps. It was already past midnight, and while the girls from The Stairway were sound asleep in a bundle of blankets behind me, I was struggling to keep my eyes open. The street in front of me was eerily deserted. A few white taxis hurtled past, and an occasional tramp would stumble by, clutching a bottle of cachaça.

For the five girls, who had recently started a new den at the top of the steps on a pedestrian precinct, it was their first night's sleep in a long time. For weeks they had been terrorised by a man who had been creeping up in the dead of night, cutting their clothes with a pair of scissors. Some of them had woken up and seen his face before he dashed off, disappearing out of sight. The gang consisted entirely of girls and without the protection of boys, was extremely vulnerable.

Often I would get a hysterical reverse-charged call in the early hours: 'Uncle, he's been here again,' one of the girls would scream. 'Please come quickly, we're scared…'

Too afraid to sleep, the Stairway girls began arriving late at the Pink House, too exhausted to take part in any of the activities. We would let them sleep during the day, curled up safely on a mat on the floor of our gymnastics room. Whenever we could Warlei and I would go late at night to their den on Alfonso Pena Avenue, Belo's main shopping street, and stay with them until dawn.

One of the girls was Glayciele, an affectionate, highly strung ten-year-old with a mop of tight, brown curls. She would always wear tight lycro shorts and tops. We began to teach her to dress in a way that would make her less vulnerable on the streets. One day Oswaldo, who worked in our family team, decided to take Glayciele to visit her mother. Arriving at the house, he found a shaky wooden shack, perched on the banks of a sewage-ridden brook. Inside the house, there was nothing but a portable gas stove and a damp mattress, covered in mould. Toddlers played on the muddy dirt floor.

'You see why I prefer the streets,' whispered Glayciele. Inside, Glayciele's mother, pregnant with her fifth child, knelt over a plastic basin, scrubbing clothes.

'There's no hope for this girl,' she nagged, pointing a knobbly finger at her daughter. 'She'd rather sleep with the tramps than here with me, her mother. I'm starting to think they mixed her up at the hospital and gave me someone else's baby.'

Glayciele's grandmother, who lived nearby, later told Oswaldo why Glayciele would constantly run away to the streets. Her mother and father, both alcoholics, would beat their daughter, leaving her black and blue. 'Sometimes her face was so swollen I'd hardly recognise her,' she recalled.

Another of the girls from The Stairway was twelve year old Poliana, nicknamed Little Chinese because of her oriental-looking eyes. She loved taking part in hairdressing classes, taken by Dora, the bubbly owner of a nearby hair salon, who volunteered her time for two afternoons per week. At 5 pm, when the house closed, Poliana would stay on, reluctant to go back to the streets with the rest of the girls. Instead, she would sit and watch television until we locked up for the night. She would talk fondly about her mother's cooking, and especially missed her younger brother and two-year-old sister. Poliana was too embarrassed to come with me to visit her mother and stepfather, who lived in a faraway district of the city. I eventually found their tiny shack, a single room that her mother rented from her sister. Inside the dimly lit room there were two beds, a rusting cooker and a kitchen cupboard. As well as her mother and stepfather, the room was also home to Poliana's two brothers and baby sister. Poliana's mother was an upright, dignified woman who disapproved of her daughter's scandalous dress sense.

'I used to tell her that she looked like a prostitute. But she would just ignore me, and run away from home,' she complained. Her parental advice could have been a little better worded, I suggested. Poliana's mother made her meagre living scavenging for rubbish at the nearby council tip. Her home was clean and tidy, although she apologised repeatedly for it.

'I don't know what to do with Poliana,' she said. 'I rarely sleep at night. I lie awake thinking about her, on the streets, getting up to no good. I worry a lot.'

Poliana also clearly loved her mother, but bridging the rift between them was not going to be easy. The more time she spent away, the harder it was for Poliana to venture back home.

'Tell her I miss her,' Poliana told me, back at the Pink House. 'And that one day I'll go home. But not yet.'

One morning Warlei and I arrived early at the Pink House, and found little Glayciele huddled up tightly on the steps of the house. Her head was buried in her lap, and she trembled and whimpered. I crouched down at her side.

'Why are you crying?' I asked, putting my hand on her shoulder. She flinched away, coiling up even tighter. As we unlocked the door, she rushed inside, locking herself in the downstairs toilet.

We discovered later, from the girls from The Stairway, that Glayciele had been raped early that morning. Camila had woken in the early hours, finding Glayciele naked, staggering aimlessly around the deserted street in front of the shopping centre. Once they had dressed her, she ran off, coming to stop at the entrance to the Pink House. It was the only place where she felt safe.

We took Glayciele to live with her grandmother, who smothered her with love and attention. This made all the difference. Visited on a regular basis by our family team, Glayciele started at school, never again returning to the streets.

Richard Wallis, from a charity in the UK, had come to Belo Horizonte to see the project for himself. On Saturday, we had been walking around the city and arrived back at the Pink House, which was closed at weekends. Regina, a fifteen year old street girl, was curled up asleep on the pavement in front of the house, sucking her thumb like a baby. In her other hand she clutched a homemade pipe used for smoking crack.

I sat down at her side, and tried to wake her. She began to stir.

'Regina,' I said quietly, 'what are you doing here, in the middle of the pavement?'

Regina opened her eyes and squinted. 'Oh, Uncle, it's you. I'm waiting for the house to open.'

'But Regina, it's Saturday. The house doesn't open until Monday.'

Regina sat up, and looked at me. As she did so, tears began to well up, trickling down her dirty cheeks. Regina's nickname on the streets was Thinny, because her excessive crack smoking had sucked her to the bone.

'Oh, Uncle Matt,' she sobbed, 'I'm missing my mother so much. It's been so long since I saw her.'

She showed me the metal pipe, covered with silver foil. 'If it wasn't for this, I wouldn't be here. I'd be at home with my mother, not lying here on the street.'

'Do you want to phone your mother?' Regina's eyes lit up. 'Yes, Uncle, I would.'

I unlocked the house, taking Regina into the office. She knew by heart the number of a public telephone near her mother's house. I dialled and passed the handset to the anxious Regina.

'Mother?' she spluttered. 'I…' Regina burst into tears, as did her mother on the other end of the line. 'I want to go home.' She listened for a moment, then cried all the more, passing back the handset. I arranged with her mother to take her straight back home.

'What should I do with this?' I asked, picking up the crack pipe.

'Throw it,' sniffed Regina, managing a smile. The waste bin rattled as the pipe landed inside.

Regina's house was in a small favela on the side of a main road, close to the city centre. We squeezed through a tiny alleyway, arriving at a tiny brick shack, an open sewer trickling past the door. Her mother was waiting there expectantly, and hurried up to Regina, giving her a long, tight hug.

Stepping into the house, Richard and I were stunned. There were no windows, as the house was closed in by other buildings at every side. The flickering television set, its power cable hanging dangerously from the ceiling, was the only source of light. A group of tiny children sat glued to the set, watching cartoons. Regina's mother invited me to sit down.

I perched on the edge of the bed. 'How many children do you have, Senhora?'

'Ten,' she replied. 'The youngest is two, then three, four, five, six, eight, ten, eleven and twelve. And then there's Regina, of course.'

There was no toilet, no sink and no shower. Apart from the shaky wooden bed and an old cooker, the dark room was empty. The children squatted on a dirt floor.

'I want to thank you for bringing Regina back,' continued her mother. 'She's always been my favourite child. She used to stay at home, go to school and help me around the house. But since she started on this *noia* thing, she just doesn't stay still any more. She suddenly takes off, and never comes back. I get so worried, I'm not eating properly. It's making me ill.' Her mother was obviously a well-intentioned woman, struggling to raise her children in terrible circumstances.

Richard was also very affected by what he saw, suggesting that we find the money to renovate Regina's house, there – by helping her mother and providing an incentive for Regina to remain at home.

Three days later Regina ran away from home, and was back on the streets. 'This street boy turned up one morning with a wallet in his hand,' her mother told me. 'She didn't even stop to put on her shoes or say goodbye.'

I knew exactly where to find her – in the playground at Pylon Hill, puffing frantically on another crack pipe. 'I'm sorry, Uncle,' she said. 'I love my mother, but I can't fight the *noia*. It's much stronger than I am.'

Later, back in England, Richard found a family who donated the money to reform Regina's house. We divided the house into four rooms, two bedrooms, a kitchen and a toilet with shower. We also put in a concrete floor, electrics and plumbing. For the first time the house had an iron door, with a lock and key. When we handed over the house, Regina's mother was speechless with gratitude.

In the pouring rain, I drove Richard to the bus station, where he would take the coach back to Rio de Janeiro to catch his plane. Arriving at the bus station car park, we met with Pamela, one of the small girls from the gang at The Stairway. She had been loitering around the car park, begging for money.

'Can I help carry Richard's bags?' she asked.

'Of course,' I said, 'but let's wait until the rain stops.' We sheltered inside the bus station, returning to the car after the rain had died down.

As I opened the boot, a gloved hand tapped me on the shoulder. I quickly turned around. It was a policeman.

'Where are you taking this girl?' he asked, pointing towards the barefooted Pamela.

'Nowhere,' I replied. 'I work with the street children.'

51

'Why, then, were you putting her in your car?' he demanded.

'She was just helping carry the bags,' I tried to explain.

The policeman did not look at all convinced. 'I think you both had better come with me.'

We were held for nearly an hour at the police post, inside the bus station. I had left home without any proof of identity, which in itself is an arrestable offence in Brazil. I also did not have any way of proving that what I was saying was true. It was ten minutes before Richard's bus was due to leave, and the policeman was quickly losing his patience.

'I'm going to call the chief police officer,' he announced. 'He'll sort this out.'

A few minutes later, the chief officer arrived, a tall, burly figure with a bushy moustache. He looked at me, and offered me his hand.

'A pleasure to meet you!' he exclaimed. 'I saw you on the TV the other day. It's a very beautiful work that you do. Well done.'

I had appeared on a national TV chat show a few nights before, talking about the work at the Pink House. The other policeman tried to cover his embarrassment and offered his apologies.

'Sorry about the mix up,' he said. 'You're both free to go.' We left the police post, sprinting to catch Richard's bus.

It was certainly a dramatic finale to his week-long visit to Meninadança. Richard looked rather shell-shocked as we waved him off.

'Bye, Uncle Richard!' called Pamela, as his bus pulled out. 'Come back soon'.

The Escape

'And call upon me in the day of trouble; I will deliver you, and you will honour me.'
Psalm 50:15

Undeterred by my adventures in Brazil, I began to prepare for my first trip to Rwanda. The Rwandan Genocide was a genocidal mass slaughter of Tutsi and moderate Hutu in Rwanda by members of the Hutu majority. During a hundred day period from April 7 to mid-July 1994, an estimated 800,000 to 1,000,000 Rwandans were killed out of a population of just over 7,000,000. These awful statistics speak for themselves.

I am rarely fearful but I was exceedingly so as I set off for Heathrow for this brief visit to Rwanda. I was going with a mission partner and as we checked in at the airport, he could not find his tickets. I thought he was about to chicken out. But after rummaging through his luggage for some time, he found them and we were on our way to Kigali.

I had been invited to Rwanda by Nathan Amooti whose parents had been refugees in Uganda after a previous and less documented slaughter in Rwanda. Nathan was raised in a remote village in western Uganda where as a boy he looked after cattle. He was sponsored through school by a lady who lives in Wellingborough and at a young age became head of a primary school in Kampala. Then he returned to Rwanda after the genocide where he was appointed by Archbishop Kolini as a Diocesan Education Officer. Nathan had stayed at our house during a brief visit to the UK and I immediately warmed to him – he has a wonderful sense of humour

*and an infectious laugh. So I thought I should accept his invitation
to Rwanda.*

*I arrived five years after the genocide but the country was still
in trauma. This is not the place to share all I experienced on that
trip but I do recall visiting a church about thirty miles south of
Kigali where there were still skeletal bodies in the building – an
estimated 5000 people had been slaughtered in this church. On the
same day, I met Stephen Gahini. He told me that he had lost 100
cows during the genocide. When I returned to the UK, I met a
farmer who donated a cow to Stephen. What amused me is that
Stephen called the cow 'Richard'. Since then we have become good
friends and he learnt English so that we could chat together on my
visits to Rwanda*

*In 1998, Stephen was ordained as a priest and since those
days when he faced the full terror of the genocide, he has developed
a diverse ministry, including reconciliation, pastoral care, working
in prisons and ministering to the military. He seeks to unite on both
sides of the historic Rwandan divide. As Archbishop Kolini says
'Not unlike Christ would seek to do, Stephen is a pastor to everyone,
beyond his own painful past'. Today, he is an Archdeacon as well as
pastoring a rapidly growing church.*

Mary Weeks Millard tells the story of Stephen in her book
After Genocide –There is Hope. *I have selected chapter 7 of
this book called 'The Escape'. This is followed immediately by the
short chapter* The story of Mary Izajiriza *which is an extract
from* Rwanda –Rising from the Ashes *by John Miles. This
needs no introduction except to say that I visited Nyamata village on
that first trip to Rwanda.*

The purpose of this book is not to give a factual account
of the history of those days, but to share the thoughts,

feelings and experiences of one man caught up in this utterly demonic madness. Most of what is described in this book about the genocide comes from testimony from people who lived in the district of Bugesera, south of Kigali. Atrocities were taking place all over the country. There was no hiding place for any Tutsi, anywhere. The massacres were the most horrific in the districts which held the greatest concentration of Tutsi people. Bugesera came into this category.

"The worst day was April 6th 1994," said Stephen to me. My interpreter, Pastor Jean-Paul, nodded in agreement. Both men were silent for a few seconds. This is a date forever imprinted on the minds of the survivors. Then Stephen continued: "Even though there had already been genocide happening in Bugesera since 1992, now all hell broke out. You must know, it was not all sparked off by the plane crash and the president's death, it was planned, it was all planned. It really started in 1992, but now the trigger had been pulled to initiate wholesale slaughter. We knew it was the beginning of the end for us Tutsis. Nothing would stop the carnage once it had begun."

Stephen knew he had to try to get his family to safety. He could not delay any longer. With a great sense of urgency, on 7th April, he at last managed to persuade his elderly mother that she would be strong enough to walk through the bush to Burundi. It was their only hope of survival, and they knew it was a very slim one. If they stayed in their homes then they would be found and slaughtered without any doubt. So they quickly prepared themselves, knowing they would have to travel light, but not knowing how long they would have to be away from their homes. They had to leave the precious cows, hoping maybe it would be all over and they could return in a few days. It was safest to travel by night because the Interahamwe, a Hutu paramilitary organization, were less active in those dark and cold hours, so Stephen collected about thirty-five of the immediate family together, and they set off, carrying very little with them. It is not easy to negotiate the bush by night, but most Rwandese would be at home eating with their family, and not many Hutu would be roaming around the countryside and likely to see them or betray them. April is the rainy season, and Rwanda's 'winter'. It was quite cold, especially for the elderly and the small children. Stephen and Francine by now had three children. They planned how best to travel. Francine carried the youngest, a baby daughter, on her back, and Stephen's sister put their one year-old daughter on her back. The five year-old son, Claude, was big enough and strong enough to be able to walk alongside them.

The family kept as close to each other as they could, hardly daring to speak. Their mouths were dry with fear. They could only wonder what the night would hold. They prayed they would make it to the border in safety. They travelled, holding on to the fact that the Lord loved them, and knew all about their situation. They were a family where prayer mattered, and they had prayed before they left, committing themselves and each other into the hands of God.

It seemed as if they were doing so well, even though they were tired, cold and hungry. Stephen estimated they had only about another thirty minutes to walk before they reached the safety of the border, when suddenly they were surrounded by an ambush of government soldiers and Interahamwe, who at once opened fire on the group. Instantly it was mayhem, screams from the injured and dying, anyone who was able fleeing into the bush, no one knowing where anyone else was. Six of those who managed to run into the bush were quickly caught by the Interahamwe and frog-marched all the way back into their village, only to be killed there by their tormentors. They hacked them to pieces with machetes and beat them to death. Only five of the group had escaped the slaughter, but at that point in time Stephen did not know what had happened to anyone else or if there were any other survivors. It was total panic and disarray. The new day was dawning; the raid had been timed for then, so that any escapees would be seen and caught by the Interahamwe as the daylight increased. Once the soldiers had recaptured the six they believed they had caught everyone who ran away and that all others in the party must now be dead, so they retreated.

Stephen had managed to run and to hide in the bush. What should he do now? As far as he knew, the killers had gone. His silent prayers reassured him and he felt convinced that he should continue alone and still try to get to the Burundi border post. In order to do this, he had to retrace his steps and return to the place of the massacre, to get on the right path again. In great fear and trepidation, in case there was a trap laid for anyone who might have escaped, he made his way back to where they had been ambushed. As he drew near, he looked carefully and listened for any sound that might indicate soldiers were still there. The coast seemed clear. Stephen could hardly bear to even look where his family lay on the ground. He wanted to just get past the place as quickly as he could, but he thought he heard a baby's cry. He listened again and, yes, a baby was crying, so he edged his way over to where the bodies were lying. In horror and shock he searched through them, gently trying to find where the baby was. Then he came upon the body of his sister, and found that his baby daughter was still alive, strapped to her back. It looked as if the baby was uninjured, and he managed to untie the cloth which held her, and lift out his baby. He held his tiny daughter and quietened her. He praised God she was safe and unhurt.

Stephen then decided that, before he left for the border, he ought to look and see if anyone else was alive, so he continued to move from one bloodstained corpse to another. It was heartbreaking to see them lying there. His eyes were nearly blinded by his tears as he identified one after another. He could do nothing for them, not even bury them. Stephen had to move quickly and quietly, for at any time the killers could return.

It was then that he saw his son, Claude, blood spattered all over him, and he was sure that he was dead. He had been shot in his arm . Stephen went to walk away when he felt that eyes were looking at him. He sensed a voice telling him to go back, so he obeyed the inner voice and walked back to Claude, and he spoke to him saying, "Little man, do you know me?" for he was sure he was dead.

But the boy answered, "Yes, you are my Dada." Claude was still alive! Praise be to God! Now Stephen had to think how he could take his two children the rest of the way. Claude was severely wounded, and the baby very tiny. How could he carry them both? He realised he could manage if he carried the baby on his back in the traditional way that the women did.

Stephen then retraced his steps and took the kitenge cloth from his dead sister's back, and with it he tied the baby on his own back, so that he could then carry Claude on his shoulders. He had to leave everyone else unburied, even his old mother, and hurry away towards the Burundi border. Claude kept begging for a drink of water. Stephen had nothing to give him. His son was very weak because he had lost so much blood from his injury. He kept crying so much that, in spite of all the dangers involved, Stephen bent down and scooped up rainwater from a puddle, in order to quench the boy's thirst. Claude drank from his father's cupped hands.

"It was a miracle," commented Stephen, "that he didn't die from drinking that water! Even the doctor in Burundi said that!"

Again, Stephen paused for a few moments, and then said, "It is my testimony that in difficult times God is always with us."

"I had to go slowly. I could not run with the baby on my back and the child in my arms. It was daylight by now, and I tried to keep under cover as much as I could as I made my way through the bush. I was relieved when I could see the border ahead, about three hundred metres away, and the soldiers there. We had almost made it to safety! My heart really lifted; I believed we would get to safety. Then I heard a noise and saw some more Interahamwe. It was a cruel blow!

"Had we made it this far, only to be killed now? I could not run because of the children, but saw a large bush nearby and crawled into it, as quietly as I could. By some miracle the children were quiet, not crying with pain or hunger. The Interahamwe had indeed seen me with the children, but thought I had run away down a small path, and they went off that way to capture me. I waited a few moments until they were safely out of sight, then as quietly as I could I climbed out of the bush. I walked as fast as I could, carrying the two children, almost at a run, and reached the border."

As soon as Stephen reached the border post, the Burundi soldiers at the post came to his rescue. They reached out to him and Stephen knew he was safe! Alleluia! He had crossed the border to Burundi!

The relief that swept over Stephen at that moment was enormous. He had reached a place of sanctuary, and the strong arms of the soldiers guarding the border reached out and took Claude from him. The little boy was still alive, but very weak from the loss of blood and also very traumatised. Amazingly, the little girl on his back had come through the terrible ordeal without being harmed. Stephen was almost naked, his few clothes torn to shreds and covered with blood.

He had no money, no possessions at all. Everything had been lost when they were ambushed. He was completely destitute, and, as far as he was aware, only he and the two children had survived the massacre. His mind was tortured by the memories of seeing all his family dying, the screams, the blood, the sheer raw terror of it all. Now he was a refugee, but the Lord had protected his life as he had promised.

The soldiers took Stephen and the children immediately to a nearby clinic for first aid. Claude needed major surgery, so he was transferred to a large hospital further into Burundi. The separation from his father just added to the terror and trauma the little boy was experiencing. Twelve years later, this young man is still suffering from the effects of those terrible days that scarred him mentally and physically.

Stephen and his small daughter were taken to a refugee camp in north east Burundi. Once registered, he found that Francine had also somehow been able to escape from the ambush, and had managed to reach the border and the safety of the refugee camp, with their other daughter on her back! The Lord had saved the five of them! They had nothing else in the world, but they still had each other. They were the only survivors from their group who tried to leave Rwanda that night.

The story of Mary Izajiriza

The remarkable story of Mary Izajiriza is not unique in post-Genocide Rwanda, but it is included here because it does powerfully illustrate the most important change in the new Rwanda. Nowadays, Mary farms her small plot of land in Nyamata village in the Eastern Province, fifty kilometres from Kigali. Aged fifty three she lives with her three surviving children; the oldest is twenty one. She is a genocide survivor.

Seventeen years after the events, she vividly remembers the day the Genocide caught up with her family and she watched as her husband and four of her children were hacked with machetes, thrown into a pit and left for dead. In the chaos she managed to run with one child on her back. Her house was burned and the cattle stolen by her immediate neighbours with whom they had lived for years. She fled to the forest and travelled only at night when most of the Interahamwe were drunk and raping women and small girls.

Eight days later she learned that her husband and four other children were dead. She says that that was the time she lost the will to live. She no longer feared death; she thought it might come any minute. After four days and nights of horror she made it across the border into Burundi where she was reunited with her other two surviving children. Mary was traumatised and lost the desire to bathe or eat.

After the Genocide she was repatriated to Rwanda.

She says 'I could not socialise with anyone, there was no more love left in me and I treated everyone like animals.' Then she was helped by the Christian Prison Fellowship of Rwanda's Director, Gashagaza Deo, who was preaching to the survivors. The survivors were taught the word of God and the need for forgiveness and reconciliation. Gradually, with God's help she was able to forgive those who had killed her family members.

One of her next door neighbours, Leonard Rucogoza, confessed to taking part in killing her family and was sent to jail, where he apologised and asked for forgiveness. He said 'I am one of those who committed the Genocide. I was imprisoned in 1995 and Pastor Deo found me and others in jail and preached the Gospel to us. I wrote to my victims and apologised. On 5th January 2005 I was released by a Presidential pardon.' At first he had to go to a training camp to prepare for life back in his village.

He confesses that he was scared of reprisals when he returned, but no one attacked him. Gradually he was able to face his neighbours and resume normal life and, amazingly, lives next door to Mary Izajiriza again. Mary now says, 'He is the first person I go to when I have a problem.' This is the power of the Gospel of Christ bringing reconciliation to the new Rwanda.

The Greatest of These is Toilets

'There is a time to laugh'
Ecclesiastes 3:4

After the success of Stories from around the World *and* Stories from around the World 2, *it was decided in 2004 that a third book should be published to make the series into a trilogy. I was told the book would be called* Funny Stories from Around the World *and decided to write a chapter on some of the toilets I have encountered while on mission. But after writing the chapter and submitting it, I was told the title of the book had been changed to* Funny and Inspiring Stories from around the World. *Whilst my chapter sought to be largely amusing, to my dismay other chapters in the book seemed to be full of inspiring stories. There was little I could do about it except ask that the following was put in the writer's profile page at the end of the book 'Richard is a focused person who cannot help laughing at himself'. And as I reread this chapter after many years, I still smile. I hope you do too.*

After I left Rwanda in July 1999, I travelled to Uganda and linked up with and led a team from the UK where we spent three weeks based on the northern shores of Lake Victoria. It was an intergenerational group with ages ranging from 14 to near retirement. And it proved to be a wonderfully harmonious and enjoyable three weeks. This short story comes from that trip.

And now these three remain: spiders, snakes and toilets. But the greatest of these is toilets.

You will never forget your first encounter when on

mission in Africa. For some, it is the western style toilets proudly displaying the Royal Doulton logo but with a flush mechanism that died a generation ago. Worse, there is no toilet brush or bleach in sight. For others, it is the tentative first steps into the pit latrine. First, you are cautioned being a new recruit – "Do not spray DOOM (the mind-boggling name for an African insect killing spray) down the hole as an army of cockroaches will emerge!" Then you go through the technique: put on flip flops, squat (I have found stretching out arms to nearest walls helpful) followed by the aiming skills of a Lancaster Bomber pilot. Swill surrounding area with a bucket of water and brush everything down hole. For me, my first encounter with a pit latrine was to prove to be a love affair. Such a simple and uncomplicated form of satisfaction.

I want to tell you a story of ghosts in white canvas, flying white teeth in a banana plantation and the official opening of a pit latrine.

The story begins with the team from the United Kingdom waking up on the shores of Lake Victoria. We had been asked to be ready by 7am and stood together in awe as dawn broke over the lake. We were ready. Many of the team had been up late preparing messages for the convention we would travel to in Western Uganda. At 10am, we were still ready and waiting and feeling extremely hot. Eventually, a battered coach came to collect us. We were on our way – or were we? First to a depot to collect our tents. I had seen cannons from the Battle of Balaclava in England (there is one near Huntingdon station) but had no idea what happened to the tents from the Crimean campaign – until now. As we crammed

65

piles of faded white cloth, twisted rope, wooden poles and cracked pegs into the pick-up that would follow the bus, I realised what had happened to them. Now we were really on our way. Choruses boomed out of the coaches windows as we headed west.

Team leadership is never without complications – today it was young Lesley, with a rapidly swelling thumb, which had been bitten by an insect. We would need to find a clinic when we reached Mbarara. We parked up in the market square on arrival at 4pm. Mary Anne, who was acting as team nurse, Lesley and I went in search of the nearest clinic, leaving a wilting team in the bus. Found a clinic. Queued to see a doctor, then the diagnosis, an injection and queued to pay the bill. Suddenly, night had fallen. How was the rest of the team? Was the bus still in the market place? For sure, morale would now be low in the stuffy bus – and it was more than fourteen hours since I had roused the team before dawn. This was my moment. Drawing on the best of Shakespeare, Churchill and St Paul, I prepared an inspiration speech to deliver from the steps of the bus. 'Once more unto the breach dear friends, once more ... we will never give up ... we must finish the race.' I strode with purpose across the market place towards the bus – Top Gun style. There comes a time in every leader's life when he must deliver. This was my moment.

'Hi Richard, we have had a brilliant time here – just amazing' was my greeting from the first group of team members I bumped into. 'Oh really?' I retorted. 'Yes, we have been sharing the gospel with folk in the market place and some have become Christians.' Double take. Who needed a morale booster?

The journey continued in the darkness. The convention was planned to start at 3pm and we would not reach our destination until nearly 9pm. Our dirt track took us through one banana plantation after another. At last, we saw the light of a hurricane lamp – we had arrived. Exhausted, we got off the bus and the first team members to descend thought they were hallucinating – they were greeted by a colony of white teeth. It was pitch black (no electricity for miles) and teeth was all they could see. As our African hosts saw our confusion, their teeth parted into huge smiles.

The story should end here – 'they slept happily ever after'. But this is Africa! Drums were beating in the valley below.

The priority was to erect the tents which the 'boy scouts' in the team attempted to do by the light of the bus's main beams. But the instructions had been lost between the Crimea and Uganda, everything was tangled up, like a pile of fishing nets, and poles did not fit holes. The 'boy scouts' started drifting all over the banana plantation as they struggled with the tent over their heads – ghosts in white canvas. Our African hosts must have been staggered. We were the first *mzungus* (white men) to stay in their village and they must have been amazed by our nocturnal customs. Realising that my leadership was now in danger of total disintegration (I had once felt exceptionally clever after putting up a small Wendy House) I asked about the drums in the valley. 'Ah Richard, this is the 3pm session. They are waiting for you to preach.' Sometimes God is exceptionally good. I left the team playing ghosts with a slightly spiritual: 'I am off to share the word down in the valley.'

I was the first up the following morning – we had been woken by the four hundred convention delegates prayer marching past our sagging tent at 5.30 am. My guess was that everyone else had followed my practice the previous night – and found a banana tree for their night time constitutional. But now it was morning and I am a regular sort of guy. I asked a senior pastor what was available. 'Oh, Pastor Richard, we have been waiting for this moment. The villagers have built a new pit latrine for the team in the village square. Please come and open it now.' I grabbed my flip flops and after the briefest of speeches, I entered the holy of holies. With arms stretched wide holding onto sacks inscribed USAID, I peered through the chinks in the sackcloth, observing the crowd awaiting for me to emerge.

I never did give my speech from the steps of the bus. But I did open a new pit latrine in Africa. I think God was amused by that exchange.

From Atheism to Abundant Life

'Anyone who belongs to Christ has become a new person.
The old life is gone; a new life has begun'
2 Corinthians 5:17

In 1992, Mission Possible was officially registered in Bulgaria and in the same year, Mission Possible Albania was established.

I visited Mission Possible's ministry with the Roma community in Bulgaria in the winter of 2007. Just as in Russia where we have a cohesive ministry approach integrating vulnerable children back into their families with soup kitchens, day centres, shelter homes, rehabilitation centres and a family ministry, I saw this same strategic interconnected approach in the marginalised and victimised Roma communities where we work in Bulgaria: first Mission Possible facilitates the establishment of a Roma led church followed by soup kitchens, literacy courses and job training projects. This approach has led to the transformation of the lives of those who we seek to serve and in particular the lives of Roma girls. Many Roma girls marry in their early teens, have children and are single mothers by the time they reach 20 years old. Mission Possible's approach breaks this vicious circle and their future is one of gainful employment rather than abandonment.

I have met many remarkable godly women over the years. Pastor Elvie Go in Ozamiz City in the Philippines is one such woman who will always have a special place in my heart as it was in Ozamiz that I cut my mission teeth. She lives in a huge house called The Happy House. I called it a Christian compost heap. About fifty people live in this house including ex street children, people with

69

physical disabilities and people with learning difficulties as well as some of the Happy Church leadership team. God uses them to 'fertilise' the whole area with His Good News. Each morning at 5 am everyone meets for an hour of prayer and worship – and no one dares to arrive without having mastered a series of memory verses! Elvie Go pastors a church of several thousand plus church plants and a range of ministries ranging from building homes for the homeless to a home for older people. Visiting the Happy House was always a challenging experience, but also one to be savoured.

When visiting Albania in 2008 I met another extraordinary woman. Her ministry base could also have been called the Happy House but is named The Centre of Hope, and is located in a place of poverty just outside Tirana. There is always something happening at the Centre of Hope – from Alpha Courses and Miracle Clubs for children, to conferences on learning job skills and coping with domestic violence. I was there just before Christmas and they were distributing shoe boxes shipped from the UK. It was all a bit like Kings Cross at rush hour with people walking in all directions. This ministry is headed up by the remarkable Besa Shapllo. What is extraordinary is that she was asked to head up Mission Possible Albania within a few days of becoming a Christian. Read on!

My name is Besa Shapllo and I am 63 years old. I was the youngest of the three kids in my family. I was born in Tirana, Albania, but spent my childhood in Durres which is the main sea-port of the country. I grew up in an atheist family, or so I believed, for our parents never denied God in our presence but never worshipped Him either.

When I was little there were churches as well as mosques all over the country. But in 1966, when I was in the 8th grade, the regime in power proclaimed Albania an "Atheist Country", and consequently closed them all down. Then, they went so far as to open an "Atheist Museum".

In the following school year I went to the capital, Tirana, to attend a special school for foreign languages. Most students learnt Russian, but I was in a small group learning English. Later, when I was in the third year, I began to write my name in English. "BESA" is a special word in Albanian. We say "BESA of the Albanians", which means faith and promise and much more all in one word, but I chose to use FAITH. In 1974, I began to use the word GOD in my diary. Whenever I had a problem and needed help, I would write: "God help me...!!!", though the word GOD was a forbidden word in the Atheist Albania. In my name of Besa, God had sown a seed that was to grow.

When I left school, I became a tourist guide. Once I was with a group in Shkoder, up in the north, where we took the tourists to visit our Atheist Museum. It was in this museum that I saw the first Bible in my life. It was a big Bible, it was open and the inside was cut out and a gun was placed there. They wanted to show that those who claimed to be Christians were in fact spies of other countries. In the museum there were exhibits of trials of Catholic priests who had been executed for espionage.

As time moved on, I became a school teacher and married. At that time we had a black and white TV, but we could watch only one station being Albanian TV, which was state owned. Once as we were watching a movie which was in English with subtitles in Albanian, we noticed that the word GOD was not translated. So that became the topic of a secret discussion between my husband and myself (you could never discuss such issues with other persons during those days): "Are they so much afraid that they do not even translate the word GOD?" we pondered.

1991 brought about the fall of communism in Albania. We were amazed as angry people gathered in the main city square of Tirana pulling down a very tall monument of Enver Hoxha, our dictator. At that time, I was just starting a journey with my husband to New Zealand, having been invited there by a New Zealand couple for whom I had interpreted. Our plan was to visit for just three weeks, but the Albanian community in New Zealand encouraged us to stay and build a life there. I was being pulled one way and then the other. New Zealand was a place of safety and prosperity, but on the other hand my family was in Albania. And in particular my mother – who had been suffering from MS since she was 43 – needed me. So at a time when many people were fleeing from Albania, I decided to move in the opposite direction. Of course, I was fearful as we returned from an island of paradise to a land of chaos. I wrote in my diary "'My God, what's going to become of us?" I was not a Christian – though in New Zealand I had encountered a Bible for a second time and this one I had opened a few times, even though I could not understand it at all.

Of course looking back, it is very clear that the Lord was leading me home to Albania. Back then I had no idea what God was preparing for me. Now I can see that just when I was feeling utterly down, He picked me up to never let go of me – and for me to never let go of Him.

The first post I received from New Zealand was an envelope from a Maori lady who I met just briefly in the home of a university teacher. There was no letter or card of greetings inside, just a small red book which had "New Testament" written on it and 'Presented by the Gideon's International' stamped inside. I did not pay much attention to that small red book back then, but neither did I throw it away. (Today it is a precious possession.) One day, as I was walking home from school, I saw a poster on the wall of Tirana International Hotel, which is right in the City Centre that said: *Learn English through the Bible.* I felt an inner desire to write to the address on the poster and ask for this English teaching course which included a full version of the Bible. After a wait of many months, I did receive the Bible from the USA – but God was not waiting that long. He was about to knock hard on my door.

By now it was late summer in 1991 and the academic year had not yet started. I went to my school to get my salary, and there I found a few of my colleagues who were curious about my New Zealand trip were asking me a lot of questions about that exotic country. They were interested as under the communist regime very few people could travel abroad. As we were talking, someone came in and announced that an American couple had arrived to visit the school. A moment later we saw a tall man and his wife and with them was a student of mine who had just graduated, who seemed to be their interpreter. As we stood up to welcome the guests, my student pointed his finger at me saying: 'Here is my teacher!' We invited them to take a tour of the school. As we were walking along the corridors, the tall man began to ask questions about my family, my husband's job, home and eventually he said: "Why don't you go to the American Embassy and ask for a job there?" "It has never crossed my mind!" I replied. "Well", he continued, "I will go there for you and ask. Give me your telephone number and I will let you know the outcome. I am staying at the Tirana International Hotel. Here is my card". As he departed, I was exceedingly dubious, asking myself why a stranger would seek a new job for me!!

Anyhow, the following evening, I was going to the opera which is located close to the Tirana International Hotel. As I was leaving the opera house, I decided to go into the hotel and ask for this man. I was feeling nervous and not sure what to expect. I had not reached the reception desk of the hotel, when I saw a man coming down the stairs. I recognized the face right away and he recognized me too. We sat down in the hotel lobby and chatted. His wife joined us a few minutes later. He confirmed that he had registered my name at the American Embassy who indicated they might call me in a few days.

We invited the couple to come for a visit in our home and the following afternoon, they arrived carrying bags filled with books. They shared about themselves telling us that they were Christians and they loved to preach the Gospel wherever they went. They handed me the books which were Bibles and New Testaments and a couple of brochures. And they talked and talked about Jesus with an enthusiasm that was totally contagious. It was one of the most beautiful evenings! Everybody felt as if we had known each other for years. Ralph and Jane Mann were lovely people, so easy to talk to and easy to open one's heart to. And I think they noticed that I was ready to receive Jesus in my heart and asked me if I was willing to take that most important step ever. I felt happy but could not find the courage to openly admit that I had already taken this decision, but I did not know how to say it out-loud. Remember that Albania was different from any other former communist country being perhaps the only country in the world where all religions were banned by law. To verbalize my new found faith was so against everything I knew.

The next day I met with Ralph Mann in the lobby of the Tirana International Hotel and while we were talking, he took me by surprise when he said: "If you are willing to accept Jesus in your life, I can help you right now." My heart was throbbing fast and I could feel my eyes moistened with tear drops. I do not remember if I said "yes", but I know that as he stretched his hands towards mine, I let him hold them and he asked me to bow my head and repeat after him. In the end I remember him saying, "God Bless you, Besa!"

We continued to spend time together, each day sharing and praying (which for me was kind of odd). Then on their last evening Ralph surprised me by saying 'Besa would you like to work for us here in Tirana, Albania? We need an Albanian to head up Mission Possible Albania. For an Albanian, you are already an old Christian"!! I could hardly utter a word. I stuttered, "I cannot quit my job as a teacher, for I love it and the school where I teach is one of the best in the country…". Ralph responded "You don't have to quit your job. Take your time and as you get familiar with your new job, you can tell us if you like it or not, if you feel you can do it…!"

I heard my voice answer "YES! I will give it a try!"

So Ralph and Jean postponed their flight home so that they could officially make me the representative of Mission Possible in Albania.

My life was turned 180 degrees round as I began my walk with Jesus. God chose Mission Possible for me to begin my new life in His Service! And it has been and it will forever be the greatest privilege for anyone to serve His Kingdom! Thank you, LORD!

Adventure in the Nyungwe Forest

'May the Lord bless you and protect you.
May the Lord smile on you and be gracious to you.
May the Lord show you his favour
and give you his peace.'

Numbers 6:24-26

(Richard's father prayed this over him
whenever he left home on a long journey)

Over the years, Nathan Amooti and I worked on many projects together ranging from building homes for child-headed families to building and supporting two schools. Then just before Christmas 2011, he emailed me to tell me that he had been appointed Bishop of Cyangugu, a remote region that nestles in the south west of Rwanda with the Democratic Republic of Congo and Burundi as neighbours.

To be honest this appointment surprised me. Nathan is a pioneering visionary and not an 'establishment' figure and I knew him as the laughing singing pastor. Now I would have to call him 'Bishop Nathan'. But, of course, Nathan has not changed and is now bringing transformation to his diocese. This has led Mission Possible UK to a new ministry area and we support his ministry there through leadership training, developing a diocesan farm, providing equipment for the diocesan clinic and more.

One of the projects we support is a church growth project in the Nyungwe Forest. The Bishop wanted my wife Ruth and me to visit this area and we planned a trip to Rwanda in early September to avoid the rains. But the rains came early and on the Sunday morning it was decided to cancel the visit to Banda in the forest due to the treacherous road conditions. But at lunchtime, the message arrived at the diocesan office that over 1000 people were waiting for us. So at 1pm we were ready to leave for Banda. By this time others wanted to join us – so there were four of us squeezed into the back seat. But I knew that this was not the only reason that this trip would be uncomfortable. I had read Rwanda – Rising from the Ashes *by John Miles in which he shares Bishop Ken Barham's experience of making this same journey. I said nothing to Ruth but my worst fears were confirmed. To get to Banda from the main Cyangugu to Butare road you follow a narrow muddy track clinging to the mountainside passing occasional landslips on the way. The brilliant reward from this experience was the amazing warm welcome from the many hundreds still waiting for us when we arrived for the 10 am service at 3pm!*

Rwanda – Rising from the Ashes *is the biography of Bishop Ken Barham who was one of Bishop Nathan's predecessors at Cyangugu. As author John Miles says 'African adventures can involve pain, discomfort and stress'. And I am mindful that though travelling that road was a once-in-a-lifetime experience for me, Bishop Nathan and his team can be regularly found on it and similar roads in his diocese.*

This chapter is immediately followed by another short chapter that I wrote for Funny and Inspiring Stories from around the World. *I am not sure if in the end it was the sun that got to my head after a long walk but this story is a powerful reminder of God's sovereign care in times of potential danger despite breaking a fundamental rule in remote places – "Always stay with your vehicle."*

Whenever Bishop Ken arrived in Africa for one of his ministry trips, his usual pattern was to travel locally in a Land Rover that he had shipped out from the UK. It was equipped with poles carried on the roof rack to help negotiate small broken bridges over streams. He also carried a camp bed and mosquito net. Travel in Africa is rarely straightforward even today. Ken often encountered difficulties from poor roads, heavy rains and mechanical problems with his vehicles. Driving over mountains on rough muddy roads would be considered a dangerous occupation for most Westerners visiting this region; for Ken it was difficult, but second nature. Living and working in Africa had equipped him more than most for the difficult driving conditions.

On one such visit, he drove with a pastor to a village called Mpinga, where they wanted to build a church. Changing gear to climb up the steep hill to the site, the gearstick refused to move. He tried everything he could think of, but it wouldn't budge. It was getting late and there was no time to find alternative transport or mechanical help with the Land Rover. There was no alternative but to take out the camp bed and sleeping bag, rig up a pole to hang the mosquito net on and settle down for the night in the open air. The pastor, his son and another man slept in the Land Rover while Ken drifted into a sound sleep to the gentle sounds of the African night.

He was woken by light rain on his face at five o'clock in the morning feeling very refreshed and ready to face whatever the day had for them. At dawn one of the men set off to look for a mechanic at a local rice factory. He soon found one and returned with him on the back of a bicycle. The mechanic managed to dismantle the gear stick and found a way to get into first gear. They drove slowly down the track to the factory where the mechanic worked and he eventually managed to get them back on the road again. In those days – before the great invasion of Japanese 4 X 4 vehicles – anyone in Africa who called himself a mechanic was expected to know how to fix Land Rovers.

The Chinese had begun constructing a much-needed road from the southern town of Butare through the forest to Cyangugu. The excavations to the mud road meant that Ken had to fight his way through the deep mud churned up by their big bulldozers. This was all in a day's work for Ken and his trusty Land Rover.

A further illustration of the dangers of travelling in this particular part of Africa was dramatically illustrated in January 1987. It was an incident that no one would ever describe as 'all in a day's work'! Ken was visiting Banda, a new parish on the edge of the natural forest of Nyungwe. He was travelling with two people from England who were on their first visit to Africa, John French aged twenty nine and a courageous septuagenarian, Eila McDermot. John had been struggling with a number of difficulties and disappointments in his life and just wanted a new start as a Christian. Eila, aged seventy three, had heard Ken talk a lot about Rwanda and was very interested as her brother had previously worked in Africa. They had had good meetings on the Sunday and settled down for the night in a small mud church. Throughout the night heavy rain fell continuously. In the morning they packed up their sleeping bags and loaded up the Land

Rover with their jerry-cans, spare wheels, camp beds and personal supplies. Ken set off down the small dirt track that had been cut into the hillside to form the crude road. He had six passengers, which included the pastor Venuste Mutiganda, his Catechist, and, as so often happens in Africa, a couple of people just wanting a lift. Among these was a lady with a small baby on her lap.

This would be a tricky drive at any time with the Land Rover fully loaded. The heavy rain had turned a difficult route into a treacherous one. As they rounded a bend Ken felt the car tilt towards the river a hundred feet below. In the split second that Ken had for thought, those adverts for Land Rover, which show the vehicle's ability to negotiate slopes of forty five degrees, flashed through his mind. He pulled hard on the steering wheel with the improbable hope of somehow actually driving this Land Rover and his passengers safely back onto the narrow road.

Ken's effort was, unfortunately, to no avail. The soft soil just gave way and the vehicle began rolling. As they rolled down the hill Ken banged his head and was knocked unconscious. One of the passengers, Eila, also had a thought flashing through her mind. She was wondering why the trees they were hitting weren't stopping the vehicle from rolling. This was because, what looked like trees to her, were in fact banana plants. These are as large as small trees, but nowhere near as solid. The tumbling Land Rover ploughed them down. Though not as solid as trees, perhaps these banana plants may have had a slowing effect on their descent and prevented the vehicle's downward progress from reaching what could easily have become a fatal speed. However, it certainly didn't seem that way to anyone in the vehicle!

Another passenger, John, whose mind was also working at lightning speed, even managed to count the number of rolls the vehicle made, which was approximately five. When halfway down the hill the Land Rover hit a log, which is far more substantial than a banana plant, and the three passengers in the rear were thrown out of the back. The passengers, together with the rear door, went flying. Miraculously, the mother with a small baby on her lap was found sitting under a banana plant with the baby, unhurt, still on her lap!

The Land Rover finally came to rest on its roof in a shallow stream at the bottom of the hill. Ken regained consciousness and found himself on the passenger side, up against John who had been sitting there. Eila was sprawled across the roof, which was partly underwater, with the wheel arches above her. Ken and John managed to crawl out of the small sliding window into the mud. John pulled the window right out and then they managed to pull Eila out and had her carried up the hill by some of the local people who were gathering round. They took out all the baggage, removed the wheels and sent everything up to the road with the help of some of the onlookers. Nothing went missing; even a small calculator was safely returned to the church. Everyone had survived with only cuts and bruises. That Land Rover was one of twelve that Ken shipped from England to Mombasa and driven through to Rwanda. It was a sorry sight upside down in the stream with its wheels missing and no glass left in the windows.

Rwanda is such a densely populated small country, that there were a lot of local people who heard the drumming sound of the Land Rover tumbling down the hillside. A crowd soon gathered from the surrounding community. On seeing everyone alive, someone remarked, 'The Lord has certainly preserved you.'

Everyone was helped to clamber back up the hill to the road. John and Eila returned to the church. Ken went with Pastor Venuste to the small local market to try to find help. Providentially, there was a man visiting with a small motorbike. He agreed to take Ken to the Forestry Centre of Rangiro, which was run by a Swiss organisation, to look for a vehicle. Ken then travelled on the back of this motorbike for thirteen kilometres on the muddy track, with one foot on the only footrest and the other held out awkwardly away from the wheel. He had rescued his cameras and had one on each shoulder. The driver was wearing a large Stetson hat and Ken had to keep his head away from it. It was a very uncomfortable journey!

They finally arrived at the forestry centre and found a small Suzuki pick-up which the manager agreed to send back to the church for John, Eila and all the gear. The driver reached the place where the road had given way and saw the Land Rover upside down in the stream below. He called for people with their implements (African hoes), and with their help cut further into the hillside to widen the road.

The Pastor, (who later became the Bishop of Butare), decided that he and the two passengers would stay at the church and sent Ken, John and Eila on with the camp beds, sleeping bags etc. They were taken to a hospital at Kibogora which was run by the American 'Free Methodist' Mission, where they were patched up. The next day Ken borrowed a car and drove with John to the missionary conference centre, called Kumbya, on Lake Kivu. Eila was kept in the hospital for two days to allow her to recover for a little longer.

The reason the Pastor and his Catechist had been in the car was that they were planning to baptise John to signify his fresh start. Now Ken did it by himself. They put on their swimming trunks and waded into Lake Kivu and John was baptised by full immersion. John had never been baptised as a baby. It was a momentous experience for both of them. John announced that the dark sins of his past life now lay at the bottom of Lake Kivu. They both felt they had escaped death by God's grace and the Lord had work for them to do. So they both dedicated their lives afresh to His service.

When Ken finally arrived home to his parish of Penhurst, the churchwarden, Paul Broomhall, who himself was from a missionary family, told Ken that when he heard the report of the accident he had said, 'We can't let the work stop because of the accident, we must buy another vehicle.' In no time at all, he had put together enough funds for him to present Ken with a similar blue Land Rover.

Ken shipped the replacement out with tools and a spare new battery for his next visit, and having negotiated the customs at Mombasa and the borders of Kenya/Uganda, then Uganda/Rwanda, drove it through the Nyungwe Forest to Banda. He took with him an engineer, Patrick Foss-Smith, from the organisation 'Christian

Engineers in Development' (see **www.ced.org.uk**). Patrick inspected the sorry sight of Ken's damaged Land Rover with no glass and the bodywork bent and leaning to one side, which was by then, back at the village. Before they had left the village, six months previously, Ken had sent a note to the local Chief to tell him what had happened.

Taking the initiative, the Chief had sent a large group of his men to the stricken Land Rover. The wheels were retrieved from the village and replaced on the vehicle before it was turned the right way up. The men carried the Land Rover (which weighed close to two tons) along the river bed and up to the church. It sat there for six months and nothing was touched. Patrick the engineer, started work on the crumpled heap. He took the engine oil out of the cylinders, cleaned anything that needed cleaning in the engine and attached the new battery using 'bulldog clips'. Within a few hours, to the amazement of Patrick's enraptured audience of local villagers, the engine spluttered and started. He then drove it round the compound with a great crowd of excited children following.

They strapped up the body with ropes and drove very carefully in convoy up through the forest to Butare where Ken was based. There was no hope for the rear of the Land Rover bodywork. However, Ken had the top half of the vehicle's body removed, converting it into a useful pick-up. He left it for Pastor Venuste to use, who eventually ruined the engine by failing to replenish the engine oil or topping up the water in the radiator – a very African story!

The main road was by then, almost completed by Chinese workers. Teams of workers from China lived for some months in temporary cabins to supervise the building and tarmacing of the road which went from Butare to Cyangugu. This was part of a programme of major roads across the country connecting border posts of Uganda in the north, Burundi in the south, Zaire in the south-west and Tanzania to the east, and to Kigali, the capital of Rwanda, where all the government ministries were based.

African adventures, such as this one, involved pain, discomfort and stress. However, they were also a powerful reminder to Ken of God's sovereign care and guidance in times of danger and uncertainty. God was certainly with him in the good times and in the difficult ones too.

McDonalds for the People

It happened at precisely 9.33 am. A massive blow out. After grinding to a halt, it is the silence you notice first. Then the crowd emerge from the village – first the children pulling at the hairs of our arms followed by the men who gleefully debate our predicament. The women simply wander by with a sideways glance with loads on their heads. For this is not leafy Surbiton but rural central Africa. Within minutes, our driver had the spare tyre in place. He should have been employed in a Formula One pit stop team . He revved up the engine as he was keen to get us to our destination – a remote border region.

I had no idea how far we would travel that day – if I had, I would have insisted at that we returned to the city. The 'hiss' came at 3.29 pm. A 'hiss' is rarely the harbinger of good news and my great fear is snakes. But there was no doubting this 'hiss' – the hiss of a puncture. We were not stranded at the edge of the world – we were close to the toppling over zone! No second spare tyre; no puncture kit. This time the silence was truly deafening.

We waited on the dirt track for 30 minutes. We prayed. Then we saw the cyclist in the distance taking an eternity to reach us like the Omar Sharif on his camel in *Lawrence of Arabia*. But he was cycling east towards the 'toppling over' place – we needed to reach a settlement along the nearest tarmac road which our driver estimated as 12 miles due west.

It gets dark in this part of Africa at about 6.30 pm. My

mission partner Andrew and I decided we would make a dash for it. With a forced march, 12 miles in just under three hours is not impossible. We prayed again and set off with a purpose. As we swept through a local village with mud huts at top walking speed in the afternoon heat, we mused if there was a local religion with a prophecy that one day two middle aged mzungus (white men) would walk right though their village. What did they make of this apparition!

We were down to one small bottle of water between us. We had walked for over an hour and we could now see the horizon – no sight of any tarmac road. We walked on encouraging each other as the sun continued to beat down. More miles and then we saw our apparition. On the hillside about half a mile ahead was a lorry unloading bricks. Yet we had seen no brick buildings since the morning. But then we understood – all places must have their first brick building and today was the day.

We rushed forward to make sure that the lorry, by now approaching from a track to the left, would pass us. Being English, we stood in an orderly two man row and waved our thumps hitch-hiker style (I know it is pathetic!) The lorry roared passed – then braked and immediately stalled. There was space only for Andrew in the cab, so I was hoisted into the back of the open lorry.

The road deteriorated as we moved downhill. Imagine a fast flowing river surging over rocks – we were dry water rafting! After descending, we came to the next village. The children were carrying flags as this was election week. I was near exhaustion and tried to behave myself. I bit my tongue and remembered my age. Yet, I could not resist the temptation. Since a kid, I have had a passion to be a political candidate (you may recall from a previous chapter that I has studied politics at university) and here was my very last opportunity. I had the perfect stage –the back of an open lorry – and I had a crowd of hundreds who could not understand a word I was saying. No point in preaching the Gospel. Then I heard the words come out of my mouth, 'McDonalds for the People – vote Richard Wallis!'. The crowd cheered. I raised both hands above my head 'Mc Donald's today, tomorrow and forever'. The crowd roared. I acted Ronald McDonald and blew kisses to the children. The crowd laughed.

I will never be a political candidate but maybe God smiled that day. And for sure He proved again that He remembers His people when they feel they are toppling off the edge of the world – for as dusk came, we discovered that we were more than 12 miles from that tarmac road.

Jesus: Hope of the Nation

'If we confess our sins, He is faithful and just and will forgive us our sins and purify us from all unrighteousness'
1 John 1:9

There was a major eruption of the Mount Nyiragongo volcano on the border of Rwanda and the Democratic Republic of Congo (DRC) on January 17, 2002. Lava streamed a thousand metres wide through the DRC city of Goma. 400,000 people fled across the border into Rwanda. As it happened, I was making my second visit to Rwanda the following week and when people heard about this volcano, emergency aid funds flowed in to equip the new refugee camps being set up in Rwanda. Visiting northwest Rwanda and Goma in the DRC had not been on my itinerary but my itinerary was going to need to change. As we progressed towards Goma, our vehicle was surrounded with two columns of refugees walking in the opposite direction. I was immediately reminded of those black and white images of people fleeing by foot from Paris in the Second World War. Crossing the border into the DRC we entered a rebellious region and to this day I am not sure who was manning the immigration post.

I spent a remarkable day in Goma – the devastation of the lava flow had the same impact as if overnight a new wide motorway had been laid right down the high street of a large town in England. And yet on the edges of this unwelcomed intrusion, normal life carried on – street traders at their stalls and subsistence farmers working on their small holdings. And to add to the strangeness of the day, we were under the protection of an armed minder allocated to us at the border crossing.

We spent the night on the way back to the Rwandan capital Kigali at Ruhengeri where I met the Diocesan Bishop John Rucyhana. But he was much more than a diocesan Bishop. At that time he was also the president of Prison Fellowship Rwanda and in time became president of Rwanda's National Unity and Reconciliation Commission. I got to know him better when I spoke at two leadership conventions in his diocese in 2006 and from time to time we would meet up in Kigali on my future visits to Rwanda. Then I heard that he had founded a remarkable new work called Transformational Ministries.

My wife Ruth and I had a packed agenda when we visited Rwanda in 2014 but I wondered if we could squeeze one more thing in. Our flight out of Kigali was on Saturday evening and nothing had been planned for that day. I suggested we took a bit of a risk and travel up to Ruhengeri (now renamed Musanze) early on Saturday morning and return directly to the airport that afternoon – a bit of a risk as road travel is rarely without some incident in Africa. So it was that we spent three brief hours in Musanze – but more than enough time for both of us to be appalled by what we saw, and realise that God wanted us to take on a new project with the Batwa people.

The Batwa people number approximately 34,000 among a population of more than ten million people in Rwanda. They claim to be the original inhabitants of Rwanda and are related to other "Pygmy" peoples of Central Africa. Traditionally they were hunter-gatherer forest dwellers with a skill in pottery.

Between 1970 and 1990 the Batwa were forcibly displaced from their forest lands without compensation. This was as a result of economic development and the creation of National Parks. They were moved to various rural areas where they now live as tenants or squatters with many of their homes being in significantly worse condition than where we would house animals. They have largely been unable to adapt to their new environment and many have become destitute turning to begging to survive. There are high levels of malnourishment and ill health.

Despite 40 years in Africa, Asia and South America, I have never seen such poverty combined with such total and utter hopelessness. We simply could not walk away and do nothing.

So partnering with Transformational Ministries we are seeking to assist 26 Batwa households (44 adults and 71 children) in 2 communities by improving living conditions, providing education for children by increasing school attendance, decreasing poverty by facilitating sustainable livelihoods and instilling positive core values into the communities to create a spirit of self-esteem. A big project? No. A realistic project for a small charity like Mission Possible UK? I believe so.

In this chapter, which is an extract from 'Jesus, Hope of the Nations' *by Mary Weeks Millard, you will read about one of the challenges facing Rwanda after the genocide. In 2002, which was 8 years after the genocide, it is estimated that about 3.5% of the population of Rwanda were either in prison or detained on suspicion of participating in the genocide. The equivalent percentage in the UK would be a staggering 2,250,000 in prison or detained – about the population of Greater Manchester. That was one big challenge. The new challenge today is integrating these ex-prisoners into communities where their neighbours were victims of the genocide.*

One inevitable result of events such as the Rwandan genocide is that afterwards the perpetrators must be brought to justice. Thousands of people were arrested and sent to prison. This was necessary for the security of the general population and for justice to be administered. By 1997 around 125,000 men and women were interned in the prisons. Every prison in the country was overcrowded and living conditions in them were appalling. Most of the prisons were old and without adequate facilities. Thousands of the prison population were Hutus who had participated in genocide, but as well as those people there was the normal prison population which would have included all three of the country's ethnic groups. This in itself could bring tensions among the inmates.

In a few prisons the overcrowding was such that there was no room for the prisoners even to lie down on the floor to sleep at night. It resulted in some of them developing such swollen ankles that gangrene developed and amputations needed to be performed in order to save their lives. It was obvious that something had to be done to deal with the problem of overcrowding. To address this the government took the measure of allowing the elderly, juveniles and the sick to be released and this eased the pressure a little. However, it immediately brought into focus a problem for the families of their victims. How should they react? How could reconciliation be achieved? There was no way that Rwanda could survive as a nation unless a way was found whereby people could be reconciled and live together once again in harmony and interdependence.

Prison Fellowship International is a global association of 110 national Prison Fellowship organisations. The groups exist all around the world and have a network of more than 100,000 volunteers who work in local prisons to help the spiritual, moral, social and physical wellbeing of prisoners. They also work with their families, caring for them and helping ex-prisoners to settle back into the community, as well as supporting the victims of crime. The work of this organisation is trans-denominational and has been widely acclaimed throughout the world.

In 1996 Pastor Deo Gratis Gashagaza accepted the post of Director of Prison Fellowship Rwanda. He had also repatriated back to Rwanda after the genocide about the same time as Bishop John, who became the President of the group PFR (Prison Fellowship Rwanda). They began to work together in the prisons to bring hope and encourage justice. In Rwanda the Prison Fellowship embraced a specialist ministry different from many other parts of the world because they had to deal with many people who had participated in genocide.

They first had to gain permission from the government to be permitted to work in the prisons, and this was granted. It was a privilege because no other religious group was offering to do this work immediately after the end of the genocide. There was no financial help available to fund the work; the men were just aware of a calling from God, a great compassion for the prisoners, and a vision that something needed to be done for them.

In agreeing to share this work, Pastor Deo and Bishop John knew they would have to travel vast distances in order to visit all the country's prisons. This in itself was a challenge as vehicles were still being hijacked and passengers murdered as they travelled in certain areas of the country. Even fuel was not always freely available, or spare parts, should repairs to vehicles be needed.

As the two men started to meet with prisoners, some of the needs began to be revealed. Many of the people who had killed others were suffering from nightmares where they constantly heard the screams of their victims, saw their faces as they cried out for mercy and their relatives' agony as they watched helplessly. How could they ever find peace again and live with themselves? Their crimes were replayed in their minds like an endless video. For some, this burden was almost too much to bear.

Deo and John also found that some of the prisoners with whom they talked had an overwhelming desire to meet any surviving victims or the families of those they had murdered, in order to beg for forgiveness. The Prison Fellowship felt it was right to organise a conference for prison directors, social workers, personnel who worked with survivors' groups and others who worked with widows' groups. After discussions, the prison authorities allowed such an initiative to be started, which gave teaching and help to both survivors and prisoners. In these discussions a way forward for both groups to find healing was explored. Volunteers were then trained to work within the country's prisons to bring the message of repentance, forgiveness, reconciliation and salvation though the grace of the Lord Jesus.

Prisoners began to respond to the teaching, and soon the government became aware of the results. It was a lifeline – an answer where there had seemed to be no answer. The government then was willing to give more help to the initiative. There is literally a 'captive' audience in a prison! Not only are people physically bound, but also spiritually and emotionally. They have no way to drown out the cries of conscience with drugs, alcohol, sex or other forms of escapism which might be used in the outside world.

The teaching focused on removing the relentless guilt of sin. The only way to regain peace of heart is by the offender taking full responsibility for the sin committed, confessing it first to the Lord, then to the world with real repentance and truly seeking forgiveness. Only when forgiveness has been received can transformation begin in the lives of those who are wounded by their sin.

It wasn't only the prisoners who needed help to find forgiveness. The survivors and the families of the victims needed help, too. Many of them had hearts which were bitter and full of hate and were seeking revenge. The last thing they wanted to do was to forgive those who had committed the atrocities! Why should they? The blood of the victims cried out for justice!

These people needed to understand that ultimately God was the judge, and He would see that justice was done (Romans 12:19). While they held such bitterness and hate in their hearts, they would become spiritually sour and these emotions would become toxic in their lives, eventually bringing sickness and constant pain in their wake, both physically and emotionally.

They would also be in a prison, one of their own making. To be free they had to be willing to forgive and give the right of revenge to God. Only this way would bring them inner healing. Bishop John and Pastor Deo began to train the chaplains and volunteers to work with the three groups. Then began the long process of reconciliation between the groups. It had to happen if there was ever to be a hope that Rwandans could live together in peace once more. This work was not just theoretical teaching; there were many practical issues to address.

Working with the prisoners and preparing them to reintegrate in the outside world, the Prison Fellowship helped those who were illiterate by holding classes to teach reading and writing. These skills would help them to find work after release. There were also sessions aimed to prepare prisoners for the changes which they might find in their nuclear families and in the wider society. Some of the prisoners' wives had deserted them and taken other husbands; others had struggled so much to survive that they had sold the family land. It was the responsibility of the prisoners' families to feed them, and this was a huge burden on some of the wives who were now left without a breadwinner to support them and their children. How could they provide food for their husbands, too?

Sometimes the prisoners had to accept the fact that when they returned home there could be children in the family who had been born to their wives by other men while they were in jail.

Before release the prisoners and volunteers discussed issues like, "How do I tell my children what I did?" They were taught that only true repentance before God and man could break the spiritual curse they had brought upon their children and grandchildren. The country's slogan at every memorial site is 'Never Again'.

This can only be achieved if the curse of genocide is broken. It is a spiritual law, clearly taught in the Old Testament, that God will bring the sins of the fathers onto the children to the third and fourth generation of those that hate Him. True repentance and confession brings not only God's forgiveness, but the breaking of the curse and, instead, the blessing of God for a thousand generations to those that love Him.

Those who feigned repentance and confession of their crimes in order to be released were likely to reoffend in some way. Some prisoners even left prison and murdered again. The prisoners had to be taught to understand these truths.

Along with repentance the prisoners also needed to understand the issues of restitution. Prison Fellowship International has a teaching model called the Sycamore Tree. In 2002 the Rwandan Fellowship adapted this scheme to meet local needs and began to implement it. Six weeks of small group discussions were held with prisoners, led by trained volunteers, followed by two weeks when survivors and family members came and shared their points of view. The discussions were based on the example of Zacchaeus, who, having met Jesus and confessed his sins, then made restitution to those from whom he had stolen.

These discussions were so meaningful that in less than six months from their institution 32,000 prisoners confessed their crimes and accepted Christ into their lives as Saviour and Lord.

In 2002 the practical outworking of this scheme began with the building of the first village of reconciliation, where released prisoners and survivors helped each other to build houses and then to live and work together. The philosophy of repentance had to be worked out in practical, social cohesion. When the houses were built and the people moved in, the new society had to continue to work together to make it an economic success. The village people worked together forming a co-operative, farming or working at some productive project together to make money and rebuild their fractured society. Only a spiritual change in people's hearts could make such a project succeed.

Bishop John and Pastor Deo took me to see one of the first reconciliation villages. We travelled deep into the countryside in the Musanze district (formerly Ruhengeri) to the village of Kimonyi. In a beautiful valley, under the shadow of the volcanoes, the village of 183 houses was built. We sat near the water pump and soon some of the villagers came to greet us. Their eyes lit up with happiness when they saw John and Deo. First some of the women came to talk, but before long they were joined by men. They came from their plantations and within minutes began to sing and dance. It was obviously a spontaneous eruption of joy and praise as they stopped work to praise God and share with us how well everything was going. Next we were joined by schoolchildren. Some of the villagers had made new marriages and families and there were now children in the community. The children of all the families play happily together.

When the village was built, each household was given a goat and a water tank shared between two households. This was an intentional policy so that, from the beginning, neighbours shared together in the matter of water management.

Although it must have been a long process to rebuild trust, the people in Kimonyi village had managed to do that and were now living as a productive community. Recently the government has brought electricity to the village and also given a grant for further development of the economy.

In all, to date, 600,000 homes have been built in reconciliation villages and each one is a thriving, productive community. The work is slow and painstaking, but it has proved that God's forgiveness and love can reunite Tutsi and Hutu again. Jesus is bringing hope to Rwanda!

The government was aware that something had to be changed in order to speed up the justice system. If the prisoners were to be tried in regular courts then it would take well over two hundred years to hear all the cases!

In Rwanda the death penalty was abolished for murder and replaced by a life sentence; however, if all the convicted murderers from the genocide had been given a life sentence, then the circle of hate would just have continued. It was decided soon after the genocide to revive the gacaca (pronounced 'gatchatcha') court system that had been used in previous generations in the villages. The idea was that the accused should be tried by the local people in the area where they had committed the crime, and the local people come forward to give witness as to whether or not there was any evidence that such a crime had been committed by that person. If the accused was also willing to confess then the sentence could be reduced by half. When this system was reintroduced it proved a reasonably successful way of trying the genocide prisoners, and although the gacaca court did not itself pass sentence, it led to some people being pardoned when there was no evidence of crime against them. It encouraged the prisoners to admit guilt, and many of those who had repented through the work of the Prison Fellowship did this, having their sentences commuted. These courts continued for some years and speeded up the justice system for many, paving the way for reconciliation.

In 2003 the government declared an amnesty for certain categories of prisoners who had confessed their crimes, and they were released to live again in peace and reconciliation. The work which Bishop John and Pastor Deo had done alongside the prison chaplains and volunteers underpinned this move, so that the prisoners really could be accepted back into the community. Of course there were some who 'confessed' without change of heart, but for many there had been a real change of heart, with repentance towards God and new life in Jesus.

For many years there had been a spiritual darkness hanging over the Great Lakes area of Africa. There have been wars and unrest not only in Rwanda, but in many of the surrounding countries. Only the gospel of Jesus can break through this darkness and bring new life and hope. It has to begin in individuals – one by one, people experiencing a change of heart. Only then can there be transformation and change in a community.

The work of the Prison Fellowship of Rwanda has been recognised by the government to such an extent that they have been asked to screen all other NGOs which have asked to work in prisons. Of course, there has been opposition from inside and outside of the Church. People question the need to continue the work so many years after the genocide. However, there is still an ongoing need for this work. There are still many people in prison whose crimes carry long sentences, and many who have yet to come to repentance and forgiveness.

Even after Bishop John's retirement he was asked if he would still continue his prison work because it was so important, and he agreed to do so. There are still around 55,000 prisoners in jail for genocidal crimes. While there are prisoners, the need for the work remains

...and finally

I hope you have enjoyed reading these few stories of what God is doing around the world. This is the first book I have written and compiled. I am told authors rarely get feedback. Please feel free to contact me on **richard. wallis@mpuk.org** Hopefully, I can take the bad with the good!!!

I am passionate about what God has called Mission Possible to do and would be pleased to speak at any church meetings. I have a reputation in my own church for talking beyond my allotted time. Apart from on one occasion in Yorkshire, that is not true! But I do speak with an enthusiasm which I am told can be infectious.

The following pages contains a brief summary of what Mission Possible UK is doing in Eastern Europe and Africa followed by ways that you can support our ministry through prayer and giving

About Mission Possible UK

Mission Possible UK (MPUK) was founded in 2007. The mission of MPUK is to advance the Christian faith by serving the poor, forgotten and marginalised through

- Serving children and families at risk
- Training Christian leaders
- Distributing Christian literature

These three objectives reflect ministries that founder Richard Wallis has worked in with several Christian organisations over many years prior to 2007.

MPUK has 10 partners and these are listed below in alphabetical order together with a brief comment.

Africa Renewal Ministries in Uganda

Africa Renewal Ministries (ARM) was founded by Pastor Peter Kasirivu in 1990. Their core vision is to develop and equip next generation Christian leaders. ARM plants churches, has a Bible College, a number of schools and a clinic. MPUK supports this ministry in several ways including conducting leadership training conferences in the south west of the country, supporting a church plant in Arua in the northwest, funding the publishing of books in the Luganda language, providing Bibles and the provision of a kitchen garden attached to a school. It was Pastor Peter who encouraged Richard to write and deliver leadership training for rural pastors in Africa which he has done in several countries over the last 12 years. This material is now available online on the **www. mpuk.org** site.

Anglican Cyangugu Diocese in Rwanda

MPUK supports the Cyangugu diocese in the remote south west of Rwanda since Nathan Amooti was appointed Bishop in 2012. This has included supporting the diocesan farm and clinic, leadership and marriage enrichment training, the distribution of Bibles and support of a church growth project in the Nyungwe Forest.

Hope and Care Association of Rwanda who run the Star School in Rwanda

Founder of the Hope and Care Association Nathan Amooti took Richard to see a plot of land on a hillside outside Kigali towards the end of 2006 with the view of building a school on it. Within weeks, Richard had been given funds to buy the land and supporting the Star School was the first project of Mission Possible UK. Today there is a 'campus' on that plot of land with over 700 pupils. MPUK supports many aspects of the school's development and has a child sponsorship programme at the school. The school has a Christian ethos and is committed to academic excellence.

Mission Possible Albania

Mission Possible Albania was established in post-communist Albania shortly after the change in the political regime. The ministry, led by Besa Shapllo, has been involved in a broad spectrum of activities, including publications, education, humanitarian aid, evangelism, and church planting. A children's magazine called Miracle is subscribed to by many thousands of children. Mission Possible Albania also operates The Hope Centre in Bathore, a poverty-stricken community near Tirana, organizing Christian activities for children, youth, and women. MPUK sends grants to support this work

Mission Possible Bulgaria

Mission Possible Bulgaria is an important local provider of Christian teaching conferences and seminars. They publish a beautiful Christian women's magazine and Christian literature. Mission Possible also partners with Roma village churches, running winter soup kitchens, providing literacy classes, conducting Bible studies and delivering vocational training. MPUK has supported soup kitchens and literacy classes in one Roma village, funded summer camps for Roma children and facilitated the publication of various books in the Bulgarian language.

Mission Possible Russia

Mission Possible has nine bases in Russia from St. Petersburg in the west through to Krasnoyarsk in Siberia in the east. These bases work with families and children at risk and the ministry includes soup kitchens, day centres, shelter homes and rehabilitation centres. MPUK supports all these ministries.

Mission Possible Ukraine

Mission Possible Ukraine is focused on the city of Odessa and the extremely poor neighbourhoods on the outskirts of the city. There is a shelter home for neglected children with abusive backgrounds and a help patrol that ministers to the everyday needs of the poor. Odessa is the hub for the Mission Possible Correspondence Bible Course. MPUK has funded an update on some of the Bible course modules and supports a new evangelism and humanitarian aid ministry in Ukrainian villages.

REMA in Burundi

REMA is a Kirundi word which means "to uplift, encourage, strengthen, console, comfort, build up, support, give hope, and recreate people who have been hit by misfortunes". Thus REMA is a Christian organisation which identifies itself with refugees and other disadvantaged people from and in Burundi. Its core ministries are peace building and reconciliation and HIV/AIDS education and care. MPUK supports both of these ministries, has conducted leadership training conferences in two provinces and distributed Bibles to several communities.

Royal Impact Ministries in Zambia

We support the ministry of Apostle Muzamai in southern Zambia. This has included leadership and marriage enrichment training, the distribution of Bibles and a job creation programme. Apostle Muzamai is on the board of a Bible College in Livingstone and we are now supporting this college.

Transformational Ministries

Under the leadership of Bishop John Rucyahana, Transformational Ministries was established to pursue the work of reconciliation in this country. In 2014, they started a new programme to support the children of historically marginalized Batwa people. Mission Possible has pledged to support this new ministry in two Batwa villages in the northwest of Rwanda until at least 2018.

How you can support Mission Possible UK

Mission Possible UK is a small mission society and any support is a huge encouragement.

News and prayer
We have a quarterly newsletter which is full of inspirational stories about our ministry and prayer requests. To receive this, please contact us – see contact details below

Giving
It would be a joy if you feel able to partner with us through giving. You can do this by

- Sending a cheque payable to MPUK to the address below.
- Clicking the donation button on our website **www.mpuk.org**
- Transferring your gift direct into our bank account:
  Sort code 40-52-40
  Account 00092063
- For regular giving, please request a standing order form by emailing or writing to address below

If you wish to designate your gift for any particular project, please let Richard Wallis know.

Mission Possible is a registered charity and you can

giftaid it

Sponsoring a child
If you wish to sponsor a child, please contact us at the address below.

Contact details
Email: **richard.wallis@mpuk.org**
Postal address: Mission Possible, PO Box 597, Huntingdon, Cambs PE29 6ET
Website: **www.mpuk.org**

Acknowledgments

This small book has been a bigger undertaking than I had expected.

My grateful thanks first and foremost must go the writers who have contributed to this book. Without them, you would only be holding a booklet in your hands.

Thanks to those who have helped me with this book. I have relied upon their time and expertise – my brother Charles who has used his skills of nearly 40 years in Christian book publishing world, my designers Roger Chouler and Tony Fisher, my copy readers Ute Mokros and John Collinson and my wife Ruth, who was frequently bombarded by me seeking advice on the book when walking through the front door after work and trying to put away her bike!

And thanks to my friends in the Christian literature ministry who have shown enthusiasm to distribute and promote this book around the United Kingdom.

I am grateful for permission to include extracts from the following books:

- Keith Danby: *Stories around the World 2* (Authentic Lifestyle 2003) with permission of the publisher
- Keith Danby: *Funny and Inspiring Stories from around the World* (Authentic Media 2004) with permission of the publisher
- Matt Roper: *Street Girls* (Paternoster Lifestyle 2001) with permission of the publisher

- Mary Weeks Millard: *After Genocide – there is hope* (Glory to Glory Publications, 2013) with permission of the author and publisher. Available globally via Amazon Create Space at **https://www.createspace.com/4254944**
- John Miles: *Rwanda Rising From The Ashes* (Verite CM Ltd 2011) with permission of the author
- Mary Weeks Millard: *Jesus: Hope of the Nations* (Zaccmedia 2015) with permission of the author and publisher

For information about how to obtain any of these books, please contact Richard at **richard.wallis@mpuk.org**

All scripture quotations are taken, with permission, from the Holy Bible: New International Version

And finally thanks to Signpost International and Matt Roper for some of the jacket photographs. I took the others!